Walter Scot, Thomas George Stevenson

Metrical History of the Honourable Families of the Name of Scot

and Elliot

In the shires of Roxborgh and Selkirk. In two parts, gathered out of ancient

chronicles, histories, and traditions of our fathers

Walter Scot, Thomas George Stevenson

Metrical History of the Honourable Families of the Name of Scot and Elliot
In the shires of Roxborgh and Selkirk. In two parts, gathered out of ancient chronicles, histories, and traditions of our fathers

ISBN/EAN: 9783337191719

Printed in Europe, USA, Canada, Australia, Japan

Cover: Foto ©Andreas Hilbeck / pixelio.de

More available books at **www.hansebooks.com**

METRICAL HISTORY

OF THE

HONOURABLE FAMILIES OF THE NAME OF SCOT AND ELLIOT,

IN THE SHIRES OF ROXBURGH AND SELKIRK.

In Two Parts,

GATHERED OUT OF ANCIENT CHRONICLES, HISTORIES, AND
TRADITIONS OF OUR FATHERS.

COMPILED BY

CAPTAIN WALTER SCOT
OF SATCHELLS, ROXBURGHSHIRE,

WITH PREFATORY NOTICES.

EDINBURGH: Printed M.DC.LXXXVIII.—M.DCC.LXXVI.
Reprinted for Private Circulation
EDINBURGH: M.DCCC.XCII.

1369502

Prefatory Notice.

THIS SINGULAR METRICAL HISTORY of the FAMILIES of the SCOTS and ELLIOTS, "Gathered out of Ancient Chronicles, Histories, and Traditions of our Fathers, preserves many curious Traditions respecting the origin of several Branches of the Families" in Roxburgh and Selkirk-shires. It was written at the age of Seventy-three, partly in prose, and partly in doggrel verse, by CAPTAIN WALTER SCOT, Son of ROBERT SCOT *of Satchells*, a cadet of SCOT *of Sinton*, Parish of Lilliesleaf, Roxburghshire. He was born in the year 1613. CAPTAIN WALTER SCOT, in his DEDICATION to "JOHN, LORD YESTER," remarks that, "I am a Gentleman by Parentage, but my fathers having dilapidate and engaged their Estate by Cautionry, having many children, was not in a capacity to educate us at school after the death of my Grandfather, SIR ROBERT SCOT of Thirlstone; my father living in a highland in Esdail-Muir, and having no rent at that time, nor means to bring us up, except some bestial; wherefore, instead of breeding me at schools, they put me to attend beasts in the field. But I gave them the short cut at last, and left the kine in the corn, and went as a soldier to Holland under Walter Earl of Buccleugh, in the year 1629. I was at that time not full sixteen years of age, or capable to carry arms in so much a renowned regiment or company as his Honour's was. I was in no more estimation than a boy, yet waited upon a gentleman in his Honour's own company, and ever since that time I have continued a soldier abroad, and at home, till within these few years that I am become so infirm and decrip'd with the gout, which hath so unabled me, that I am not able, neither to do the king, nor myself service; so this being entered into my consideration, it is sufficiently known that my intention and meaning was not to make any profit to myself; for I know I do but little deserve, by reason I could never write a line in my life; neither will my ability keep one to write to me; and I living two or three mile from a school; yet is constrain'd by my own wilful will, sometimes to hire one school-boy, and sometimes another, yet knows not whether they can spell true Scots or not, by reason I cannot read their hand, and there is none by me that can; for many times the writer mistakes the word from my deliverence; Therefore I hope your Honour will excuse the failing of my unlearned muse."

The author then relates in the following lines that:—

"I was once a man, though now I'm none but a poor decript one;
Fifty seven years, arms did I bear abroad, or in Scotland,
When I began on the twenty ninth, I was a slender man;
Now when I end on the eighty eight, I am not very strong.
I never was an hour at school, although these lines I dite,
I never learn'd the catechism, and yet I none can write,
Except the letters of my name which I scarcely understand,
These I was forc'd to learn for shame when I was in command."

JOHN GIBSON LOCKHART, in his "MEMOIRS of the LIFE of SIR WALTER SCOTT," remarks, "That the race of the Scotts had been celebrated, however, long before his day, by a Minstrel of its own; nor did he conceal his belief that he owed much to the influence exerted over his juvenile mind by the rude but enthusiastic clan-poetry of old *Satchells*, who describes himself on his *Title-page* as

"Captain Walter Scot, an old Souldier, and no Scholler,
And one that can write nane,
But just the Letters of his name."

His 'True History of several honourable Families of the Right Honourable Name of Scot, in the Shires of Roxburgh and Selkirk, and others adjacent, gathered out of Ancient Chronicles, Histories, and Traditions of our Fathers,' includes, among other things, a string of complimentary rhymes addressed to the first Laird of Raeburn; and the copy which had belonged to that gentleman was in all likelihood about the first book of verse that fell into the Poet's hand. How continually its wild and uncouth doggrel was on his lips to his latest day, all his familiars can testify; and the passages which he quoted with the greatest zest were those commemorative of two ancient worthies, both of whom had had to contend against physical misfortune similar to his own. The former of these, according to SATCHELLS, was the immediate founder of the branch originally designed of SINTON, afterwards of HARDEN:—

"It is four hundred winters past in order
Since that Buccleuch was Warden in the Border;
A son he had at that same tide,
Which was so lame could neither run nor ride.
John, this lame son, if my author speaks true,
He sent him to St. Mungo's in Glasgu,
Where he remained a Scholars time,
Then married a wife according to his mind. . . . .
And betwixt them two was procreat
Headshaw, Askirk, SINTON, and Glack."

"But if the Scholarship of *John the Lamiter* furnished his descendant with many a mirthful allusion, a far greater favourite was the memory of

William the Boltfoot (WILLIAM SCOTT, first laird of Harden, a fierce and gallant Warrior. He was called "Willy with the boltfoot," from a lameness arising from a wound in Battle), who followed him in the sixth generation.

> "The Laird and Lady of Harden,
> Betwixt them procreat was a son,
> Called William Boltfoot of Harden;"

The emphasis with which the next line was quoted I can never forget—

> "He did survive to be A MAN."

"He was, in fact, one of the 'prowest knights' of the whole Genealogy— a fearless horseman and expert spearman, renowned and dreaded; and I suppose I have heard Sir Walter repeat a dozen times, as he was dashing into the Tweed or Ettrick, "rolling red from brae to brae," a Stanza from what he called an old Ballad, though it was most likely one of his own early imitations;

> "To tak the foord he aye was first,
> Unless the English loons were near;
> Plunge vassal than, plunge Horse and Man,
> Auld Bolfoot rides into the rear."

"From childhood's earliest hour," says the Poet, in one of his last Journals, "I have rebelled against external circumstances." How largely the traditional famousness of the Stalwart *Boltfoot* may have helped to develope this element of his character, I do not pretend to say; but I cannot avoid regretting that Lord Byron had not discovered such another 'Deformed Transformed' among his own chivalrous progenitors."

SIR WILLIAM FRASER, in his "MEMOIRS of the SCOTTS OF BUCCLEUCH," 2 vols., 4to, 1878, remarks that, "Previous to the time of Sir Walter Scott, another member of the Clan, with the same name, wrote a Metrical History of the Scotts. This History was published in the year 1688, and was written by Captain Walter Scot of Satchells,—as he is usually designated, from his being the son of the Laird of Satchells,—in the County of Roxburgh. This Work is entitled, 'A True History of several Noble Families of the right Honourable Name of SCOT, in the Shires of Roxburgh and Selkirk, and others adjacent, gathered out of Ancient Chronicles, History, and Traditions of our fathers.' The author of the 'True History' was born in the year 1613. He appears to have been the son of Robert Scott of Satchells, a cadet of Scott of Sinton, who received from John, Archbishop of Glasgow, a Charter of the lands of 'Satscheillis,' in the barony of Lilliesleaf, and Shire of Roxburgh, which narrates that Robert Scott or his predecessors had possessed the heritage beyond the memory of man. The Charter is dated 10th February 1607, and was confirmed by a Crown Charter under the Great Seal, on 14th December 1609. Robert Scott of 'Satscheillis,' also received a Crown Charter under the Great Seal, 24th

November 1609, of the lands of Dodbank, in the Shire of Selkirk, occupied by him and the late James Scott, his father, and others their predecessors, as old and native reutallers, and tenants thereof. Robert Scott was one of the pensioners of the House of Buccleuch, and he had Southinrig for his service. The Property of Satchells now forms part of the estate of Sinton. The House of Satchells was called the 'White Peel,' because it was whitewashed. No part of it now remains."

"The family estate of Satchells was so far reduced when his father succeeded to it, that young Walter had to be kept at home to herd the few cattle that still remained. But a pastoral life was not congenial to him, and, as he himself says, he 'gave them the short cut, and left the kine in the corn.' He joined the Expedition to Holland in the year 1629, where he served in the regiment raised by his chief, Walter, second Lord Scott, and first Earl of Buccleuch. When Seventy-three years of Age, Satchells composed the 'True History of the Family of Scot,' in which he describes himself as—

> "An old souldier, and no Scholler,
> And one that can write nane,
> But just the Letters of his name."

"SATCHELLS, while admitting his want of Scholarship, does not acknowledge it to be any disqualification for the work of an Historian, and, indeed, he criticises several Historians with much freedom when their opinions differ from his own. His industry enabled him to collect many facts that came within his own knowledge, and his record of these is valuable. But his history of the origin and early generations of the Scott Family is to be taken with the utmost caution. According to him, the founder of the house of the Scotts of Buccleuch came from Galloway, in the reign of King Kenneth the Third, in the tenth century. The tradition which Satchells relates is said to have been received by him while serving as a soldier. Having occasion to pass to the English side of the Border, he became acquainted with a gentleman, named Lancelot Scot, who showed him a book, said to have been written by Michael Scott, called the Wizard, and informed him that it

> "Was never yet read through
> Nor never will, for no man dare it do."

"SATCHELLS himself could not read, so that he had to depend upon his informant, who related to him the contents of Manuscript Histories concerning the origin of the Scots :—

> "But to proceed, he wearied not
> To shew the original of the border Scot,
> He said, that book did let him understand,
> How the Scots of Buckcleuch gain'd both name and land."

SIR WALTER SCOTT, in his NOTES to the "Lay of the Last Minstrel," Remarks that " BELLENDEN is situated near the head of Borthwick Water, and

being in the centre of the possession of the Scotts, was frequently used as their place of rendezvous and gathering word. Hence SATCHELLS calls one part of his Genealogical Account of the Families of that Clan, his Bellenden."
"WATTS" was a retainer of the Buccleuch Family. His name was "WATT TINLINN, by Profession a sutor, but, by inclination and practice, an archer and warrior, and held for his border service a small tower on the frontiers of Liddesdale."
There were THREE EDITIONS printed of SATCHELLS' HISTORY. The FIRST EDITION is exceedingly rare. It was published in Quarto at Edinburgh in 1688. "A perfect copy of this is in the Library of the Duke of Buccleuch at Bowhill, and another in his Library of Dalkeith House, where a third copy has also recently been found, wanting the Title page, and a few leaves at the beginning." Mr ARCHIBALD CONSTABLE, Bookseller, presented a copy "To WALTER SCOTT, Esquire, from his obliged and faithful servant, ARCHD. CONSTABLE. It is the only copy of the First Edition I have ever seen. A. C., Park Place, 24th March 1818."
JOHN GIBSON LOCKHART remarks, "That Scott's Family well remembers the delight which he expressed on receiving, in 1818, a copy of this FIRST EDITION, a small dark quarto of 1688, from his friend, ARCHIBALD CONSTABLE. He was breakfasting when the present was delivered, and said, 'This is indeed the resurrection of an old ally—I mind *spelling* these lines.' He read aloud the jingling epistle to his own Great-Great-Grandfather, which, like the rest, concludes with a broad hint that, as the author had neither lands nor flocks—'no estate left except his designation'—the more fortunate kinsman who enjoyed, like Jason of old, a fair share of *fleeces*, might do worse than bestow on him some of King James's *broad pieces*. On rising from table Sir Walter immediately wrote as follows—in imitation of his namesake's style of composition—on the blank leaf opposite to poor Satchell's honest title-page:—

> "' I, Walter Scott of Abbotsford. a poor scholar, no soldier, but a soldier's lover,
> In the style of my namesake and kinsman, do hereby discover
> That I have written the twenty-four letters twenty-four million times over ;
> And to every true-born Scott I do wish as many golden pieces
> As ever were hairs in Jason's and Medea's golden fleeces.' "

"The Rarity of the ORIGINAL Edition of Satchells is such that the copy now at Abbotsford was the only one Mr ARCHIBALD CONSTABLE had ever seen. And no wonder, for the author's *envoy* is in these words:—

> "Therefore begone my book, stretch forth thy wings and fly,
> Amongst the nobles and gentility :
> Thour't not to sell to scavengers and clowns,
> But given to worthy persons of renown.
> The number's few I've printed in regard
> My charges have been great, and I hope reward ;
> I caus'd not print many above twelve score,
> And the printers are engag'd that they shall print no more."

PREFATORY NOTICE.

THE SECOND EDITION is very scarce. It was also published in Quarto at Edinburgh in 1776, and contains what is designated "Satchels's Post'ral, humbly presented to his Noble and Worthy Friends of the Names of SCOT and ELLIOT, and others."

In the year 1830, SIR WALTER SCOTT presented to the late Mr PRINGLE *of Whytbank* a copy of the Second Edition of 1776, with this inscription on the fly-leaf:—"The gift of WALTER SCOTT to his hereditary friend, ALEXANDER PRINGLE, Esquire *of Whytbank.* Abbotsford, 14th March 1830."

Along with the book Sir Walter also wrote the following letter:—

"MY DEAR ALEXANDER,—I am the enviable possessor of the edition princeps of my namesake Satchells, so I am enabled to beg your acceptance of the Reprint of 1776, which is now scarce, and indispensable to your studies. I am very much obliged to you for the remarks on my ancestor, which I wish you would one day complete. Always faithfully yours.— WALTER SCOTT."

Mr JAMES MAIDMENT'S copy of this Edition was sold at the sale of his Library in Edinburgh in 1880 for Two Pounds and Four Shillings.

Mr JOHN WHITEFOORD MACKENZIE'S copy of the same Edition was sold at the sale of his Library in Edinburgh in 1886 for Three Pounds and Eighteen Shillings.

THE THIRD EDITION is rather scarce. It was printed in Small Octavo by George Caw at Hawick in 1786, with "Elucidations from the best Historians and Works on Heraldry." In this Edition "several notes are given to vindicate our author in opposition to some modern writers." It also contains "Notices of the Family of Buccleugh from the time of the Duke of Monmouth (1685) to the present Duke of Buccleugh (1767), with a brief Sketch of the Public Character of that Patriotic Nobleman—Henry, Duke of Buccleuch—And Memoirs of the Life, and Military services of Lieutenant-General Sir George Augustus Elliot 'The brave and Gallant defender of Gibraltar.'"

THE COPY used for this REPRINT was that of the "SECOND EDITION," printed in 1776.

THE IMPRESSION OF THIS VOLUME—The SECOND of an intended series of Reprints of rare, curious, and remarkable works pertaining to SCOTLAND—is limited to FIFTY COPIES, will, it is hoped, give satisfaction, and prove acceptable to the Subscribers.

T. G. S.

EDINBURGH, *July* 1892.

A TRUE

HISTORY

Of several Honourable Families of the Right Honourable NAME

OF

SCOT,

In the Shires of Roxburgh and Selkirk, and others adjacent.
Gathered out of Ancient Chronicles, Histories, and Traditions of our Fathers.

BY

Captain WALTER SCOT,

An old Souldier, and no Scholler,

And one that can write nane,
But just the Letters of his name.

EDINBURGH: Printed by the Heir of ANDREW ANDERSON, Printer to His Most
Sacred Majesty, City and Colledge, 1688; and reprinted by
BALFOUR & SMELLIE, 1776.

To the Right Honourable, and Generous Lord,

JOHN
LORD YESTER,

Appearand EARL of TWEDDALE; Son to Jean Countess of Tweddale, who was Daughter to that valient Lord, Walter Earl of Buckcleugh, your Honour's worthy Grand-Father.

AS the Graces, the Vertues, the Senses, and the Muses are embled or alluded to your noble sect; as all these have ample residence in your honourable and worthy disposition; to whom then but yourself, being a person so compleat, should I commit the patronage of that worthy Lord, Walter Earl of Buckcleugh; and though I am an unliterate, souldier, have not apparelled them in such garments of elocution, and ornate stile, as befits their Honours, and eminency of the least part of their excellent worthiness; yet, I beseech your Honour to accept for your own worth, and their worthiness; for if it were not but that I am assured, that your noble disposition in all parts is suitable to the in-side of this book, I should never have dar'd to dedicate it to your patronage: As it hath an honest intention, so hath your breast ever been fill'd with such thoughts, which brings forth worthy actions; as it is a whip or scourge against all pride, so have you ever been an unfeigned lover of courteous humanity and humility. I humbly beseech your Honour, although the method and stile be plain, to be pleased to give it a favourable intertainment; for records and histories do make memorable mention of the diversity of qualities of sundry famous persons, men and women, in all the countries and regions of the world: How some are remembred for their piety and pity,

a some

some for justice, some for severity, for learning, wisdom, temperance, constancy, patience, with all the virtues divine and moral. God, who of his infinite wisdom made man, of his unmeasured mercy redeemed him, of his boundless bounty, immense power, and eternal eye of watchful providence, relieves, guards, and conserves him. It is necessary that every man seriously consider, and ponder these things, and in token of obedience and thankfulness, say with David, 'What shall I render?' &c. Men should consider why God hath given them a being in this life. No man is owner of himself. My age is seventy-three; it is fifty seven years since I went to Holland with your honourable grand-father, Walter Earl of Buckcleugh, in the year 1629. I was at that time not full sixteen years of age, or capable to carry arms in so much a renowned regiment or company as his Honour's was; I was in no more estimation than a boy, yet waited upon a gentleman in his Honour's own company; notwithstanding it is known, that I am a gentleman by parentage, but my fathers having dilapidate and engaged their estate by cautionry, having many children, was not in a capacity to educate us at school after the death of my grandfather, Sir Robert Scot of Thirlstone; my father living in a highland in Esdail-muir, and having no rent at that time, nor means to bring us up, except some bestial; wherefore, instead of breeding of me at schools, they put me to attend beasts in the field; but I gave them the short cut at last, and left the kine in the corn, and went as aforesaid; and ever since that time I have continued a soldier abroad, and at home, till within these few years that I am become so infirm and decrip'd with the gout, which hath so unabled me, that I am not able, neither to do the king, nor myself service; so this being entered into my consideration, it is sufficiently known that my intention and meaning was not to make any profit to myself; for I know I do but little deserve, by reason I could never write a line in my life; neither will my ability keep one to write to me; and I living two or three mile from a school; yet is constrain'd by my own wilful will, sometimes to hire one school-boy, and sometimes another, yet knows not whether they can spell true Scots or not, by reason I cannot read their hand, and there is

none

none by me that can; for many times the writer mistakes the word from my deliverance; Therefore I hope your Honour will excuse the failing of my unlearned muse.

Seek then Heaven's kingdom, and things that are right,
And all things else shall be upon the cast ;
Holy days of joy shall never turn to night,
Thy blessed state shall everlasting last.
Live still as ever in thy Maker's sight,
And let repentance purge your vices past.
Remember you must drink of death's sharp cup,
And of your stewartship account give up.
Had you the beauty of fair Absalom,
Or did your strength the strength of Sampson pass ;
Or could your wisdom match wise Solomon,
Or might your riches Cracsus wealth surpass :
Or were your pomp beyond great Babylon,
The proudest monarchy that ever was ;
Yet beauty, wisdom, riches, strength, and state,
Age, death, and time will spoil and ruin it.
Health, happiness, and all felicity,
Unto the end may your attendance be.

Your honour's most obedient,

Humble, and devoted servant,

WALTER SCOT.

The INDEX.

PART FIRST.

CONTAINING a true History of several Honourable Families of the Right Honourable name of SCOT ; Or, a true genealogy of the renowned and Honourable family of BUCKCLEUGH	Page 3
The antiquity of the name of SCOT	p. 27
The several places of residence of the family of BUCKCLEUGH	p. 43
The gentlemen's names who were pensioners to the house of BUCK-
CLEUGH, with the lands they possessed for their service	p. 45

PART SECOND.

CONTAINING Satchel's Post'ral, presented to his noble and worthy friends of the names of SCOT and ELLIOT	p. 1

The names of the Gentlemen to whom several dedications are presented, are to be found out as follows,

Walter Earl of Tarras	p. 4
Sir Francis Scot of Thirlston	p. 8
Robert Scot second son to Sir William Scot of Hardin	p. 11
William Scot of Rae-burn	p. 13
Thomas Scot of Whitslade	p. 15
John Scot of Wall	p. 18
Sir William Scot of Hardin	p. 21
Sir John Scot of Ancrum	p. 22
Sir William Scot of Hardin younger	p. 24
Hugh Scot of Gallow-shiells	p. 26
Sir Patrick Scot of Long-newton	p. 29
Robert Scot of Horsliehill	p. 30

Captain

Captain James Scot	p. 31
James Scot of Bristo	ibid
James Scot of Bow-hill.	p. 32
Sir William Elliot of Stobs	p. 34
The Laird of Lariston	p. 34
William Elliot of Dunlibire	p. 44
Robert Elliot of Midliemill	p. 45
John Elliot brother to Sir William Elliot of Stobs	p. 46
William Elliot, uncle to the said Sir William	p. 47
Mr Gavin Elliot uncle to the said Sir William	ibid
Robert Elliot appearant of Dunlibire	p. 48
Robert Elliot appearant of Lariston	p. 49
Gilbert Elliot son to Sir William Elliot of Stobs	ibid
John Hoppringil of Torsouce	p. 50
John Riddel of Haining	p. 52
Andrew Plummer of Middlestead	p. 55
James Gladstains of that Ilk	p. 56
Robert Langlands of that Ilk	p. 57
Francis Gladstains of Whitlaw	p. 58
Walter Scot of Burn-foot	p. 59
Francis Scot, brother-german to the Laird of Burn-toot in An	ibid
Henry Forrester of Stonegirthside in England	p. 60
John Scot appearand of Headshaw	p. 61
Mr Richard Scot, Parson of Askirk	p. 62

A True History of several Honourable Families of the Right Honourable Name of Scot, &c.

I Was once a man, though now I'm none but a poor decript one;
Fifty seven years, arms did I bear abroad, or in Scotland,
When I began on the twenty ninth, I was a slender man;
Now when I end on the eighty eight, I am not very strong.
I never was an hour at school, although these lines I dite,
I never learn'd the catechism, and yet I none can write,
Except the letters of my name which I scarcely understand,
These I was forc'd to learn for shame when I was in command.
   Of shepherds swains I mind to carp,
And valiant Tammerlane into the second part,
My drowsie muse is almost drown'd with care,
How she dare venture to climb Honour's stare:
The Honour's little worth that's purchas'd by coyn,
Joan made such a market when she was Pope of Rome.
Honour hath gilded wings, and soars most high,
And does behold the steps of Majesty;
Honour the lofty lyon of renown,
Which is no merchandize for butcher or clown:
Honour's the greatest favour a Prince can yield,
All true gain'd honour is win into the Field;
He needs no complementing book him to instruct,
That gains his honour by valour and conduct;
' Peasant bought honour is like to those,
' That puts a gold ring in a brood-sow's nose:

                                          Whereas

Whereas other metal may serve as well,
Either copper, brass, iron, or steill;
I wish true honour still may be preserv'd;
For many gets honour that n'ere does deserv't :
The valiant Earl of Buckcleugh, when I was young,
To the bush in Barbant with his regiment came,
Which is the space of fifty nine years agone,
' I saw him in his arms appear,
' Which was on the sixteen hundred and twenty seven year;
That worthy Earl his regiment was so rare,
All Hollands leagure could not with him compare;
Like Hannibal, that noble Earl he stood,
To the great effusion of his precious blood;
The town was tane with a great loss of men,
To the states of Holland from the King of Spain.
His honour's praise, throughout all nations sprung,
Born on the wings of Fame that he was Mars's son,
The very son of Mars, which furrowed Neptune's brow :
And over the dangerous deep undauntedly did plow.
He did esteem his countries honour more,
Than life and pelf which peasants does adore :
' His noble ancestors their memories
' Are born on wings of Fame, as far as Titan's rise;
And universally they are divulg'd from thence,
Through the circle of all Europe's circumference :
Let their example be a spur to you,
That you their worthy vertues may pursue.
They were brave men, I wish ye be so still,
They had good courage guided with good skill,
Which skill and courage, fortune, grace and will,
I do bseeech the Almighty to bestow
On you their off-spring all, both high and low;
Time hath recorded Buckcleugh's matchless force,
By sea or land with valiant foot or horse;

He made France tremble, and Spain to quake;
The foundation of Barbant they made shake:
And as true valour did inspire their breasts,
So victory and honour crown'd their crests,
Of both Walter Lord, and Walter Earl;
In the Netherlands they did so much prevail.
I wish your good intention may contain,
And you may be like them in every thing;
That as your parents are, so you may be
Rare patterns unto your posteritie.
That all your foes with terror now may know,
Some branches of Buckcleugh has beat them so;
True Honour, Fame and Victory attend you,
And great Jehovah in your just cause defend you;
That immortality your fames may crown,
And God may have the glory and renown.

When brave Earl Walter he was dead and gone,
He left his son Earl Francis in his room;
Who married when he was but young,
' Before he came to perfection;
His age was twenty years and five,
When death depriv'd him of his life;
His Familie they were but twain,
He left them in the mother's keeping;
So by experience we see every day,
That bad things do increase, and good things do decay;
And vertue with much care from vertue breeds,
Vice freely springs from vice, like stinking weeds.
Sardanapulus King of Babylon,
' Was to his concubines such a companion,
That he in their attire, did show, and sign,
An exercise unfitting for a King:
These, and a number more his fancy fed,
To compass which his shifts were manifold:
A bull, a ram, a swan, a shower of gold,

To dreadful thunder, and consuming fire,
And all to quench his inward flames desire:
Apollo turn'd fair Daphne into bay,
Because she from his lust did flie away:
He lov'd his Hiacinth, and his Loronis,
As fervently as Venus and Adonis;
So much he from his god-head did decline,
That for a wench he kept Dametus kine;
And many other gods have gone astray,
If all be true, which Ovid's books doth say;
' Thus to fulfill their lusts, and win their Trulls,
' We see that these ungodly gods were Gulls;
The mighty captain of the Mermidons,
Being captivated to these base passions,
Met an untimely unexpected slaughter,
For fair Pollixena, King Priamus's daughter;
Lucretius rape was Tarquin's overthrow,
Shame often payes the debt that sin doth owe;
What Philomela lost, and Tyrus won,
It caus'd the lustful father eat his son;
In this vice Nero took such beastly joy,
He married was to Sperus a young boy;
And Piriander was with lust so fed,
He with Melista lay when she was dead,
Pigmalion with an image made of stone
Did love and lodge, I'll rather lie alone;
Aristophanes join'd in love would be,
' To Asheas, but what an ass was he;
A Roman Appius did in goal abide
For love of fair Virginia, where he died;
That second Henry aged childish fond
On the fair feature of fair Rosamond;
That it raised most unnatural and hateful strife,
Betwixt himself, his children, and his wife;

The

The end of which was, that the jealous Queen,
Did poison Rosamond in furious spleen;
The fourth English King Edward lower did descend,
He to a gold-smith's wife his love did bend,
This suggred sin hath been so general,
That it hath made the strongest champions fall,
For Sichem ravished Diana; for which deed,
A number of the Sichemites did bleed;
And Sampson the prime of manly strength,
By Dalila was overcome at length:
King David frailly fell, and felt the pain,
And with much sorrow was restor'd again.
Though Saul his foe he no way would offend,
Yet this sin made him kill his loyal friend;
A man with Thamar incest did commit,
And Absalom depriv'd his life for it.
And Solomon allow'd most royal means,
To keep three hundred concubines,
By whose means to idolatry he fell,
Almost as low, as to the gates of hell;
At last repenting, he made declaration,
That all was vanity, and sp'rits vexation;
Abundance of examples men may find,
Of Kings and Princes to this vice inclin'd,
Which is no way for meaner men to go;
Because their betters often wandred so:
For they were plagu'd of God, and so shall we,
Much more, if of their sin we partners be.
' To shew what women have been plunged in,
' The bottomless abyss of this sweet sin;
There are examples of them infinit,
Which I ne're mean to read, much less to writ,
To please the reader, though I'll set down some,
As they unto my memory do come.

Now I leave the familie, and return again to brave Lord Walter, *and his son* Walter Earl *in* Scotland, *where these worthy Lords were born.*

LORD of Buckcleugh into the Scots border
'Was high Lord Warden, to keep them in good order;
On that border was the Armstrangs, able men,
Somewhat unruly, and very ill to tame;
I would have none think that I call them thieves;
For if I did, it would be arrant lies;
For all Frontiers, and Borders, I observe,
Wherever they lie, are Free-booters,
And does the enemy much more harms,
Than five thousand marshal-men in arms;
The Free-booters venture both life and limb,
Good wife, and bairn, and every other thing;
He must do so, or else must starve and die;
For all his lively-hood comes of the enemie:
His substance, being, and his house most tight,
Yet he may chance to loss all in a night;
' Being driven to poverty, he must needs a Free-booter be,
Yet for vulgar calumnies there is no remedie:
An arrant liar calls a Free-booter a thief,
A free-booter may be many a man's relief:
A free-booter will offer no man wrong,
Nor will take none at any hand;
He spoils more enemies now and then,
Than many hundreds of your marshal-men:
Near to a border frontier in time of war,
There ne'er a man but he's a free-booter:
Where fainting fazard dare not show their face;
And calls their offspring thieves to their disgrace;
These are serpents spirits, and vulgar slaves,
That slanders worthies sleeping in their graves.

But

But if fourty countrymen had such rascalls in bogs,
They'd make them run like feltered foals from dogs;
The Scot and Ker the mid border did possess,
The Humes possest the east, and the Johnstons the west,
With their adjacent neighbours, put the English to more pains,
Nor half the north, and all three Lothians:
Yet with the Free-booters I have not done,
I must have another fling at him,
Because to all men it may appear,
The Free-booter he is a volunteer;
In the muster-rolls he has no desire to stay,
He lives by purchase, he gets no pay:
King Richard the second of England sent,
A great army well arm'd into Scotland,
Through Cumberland they came by his command,
And ordain'd to cross the river at Solway sand.
In Scotland King Robert Stuart the first did reign.
'Yet had no intelligence of their coming;
The Free-booters there they did conveen,
To the number of four or five hundred men:
In ambush these volunteers lay down,
And waited whilst the army came;
At a closs strait place, there they did stay,
Where they knew the English could not get by-way;
And when they came the ambush nigh,
They rose with clamours and shouting high:
Which terrified the English men,
That they drown'd most part in Solway Sand:
It's most clear, a Free-booter doth live in hazard's train,
A Free-booter's a caveleer that ventures life for gain:
But since King James the sixth to England went,
There has been no cause of grief,
And he that hath transgressed since then,
Is no Free-booter, but a thief.

In Queen Elizabeth's reign she kept a strong garrison,
At Carlisle, that sink-port,
Of horse and foot, a thousand men compleat,
The governor was the Lord Scroup,
It fell about the Martinmass, when kine was in the prime,
Then Kinmont Willy, and his friends, they did to England run.
Oxen and kine they brought a prey out of Northumberland,
Five and fifty in a grift, to Canninbie in Scotland:
The owners pityfully cry'd out they were undone,
Then to the governor they came, and seriously did complain:
The Lord Scroup heard their whole complaint,
And bad them go home again, and no more lament,
For before the sun did rise or set,
He should be reveng'd on Kinmont:
Anone he charged the trumpeters, they should sound Booty-saddle,
Just at that time the moon was in her prime,
He needed no torch light:
Lord Scroup he did to Scotland come,
Took Kinmont in the self same night:
If he had had but ten men more, that had been as stout as he,
Lord Scroup had not the Kinment tane with all his company;
But Kinmont being prisoner, Lord Scroup he had him tane,
In Carlisle castle he him laid, in irons and fetters strong:
Then scornfully Lord Scroup did say,
In this castle thou must lie,
Before thou goest away, thou must
Even take thy leave of me;
He mean'd that he should suffer death before he went away;
By the cross of my sword says Willy then,
I'll take my leave of thee,
Before e're I go away, whether I live or die;
These news came forth to bold Buckcleugh,
Lord Warden at that time,
How Lord Scroup Carlisle's governour
Had Kinmont Willie tane;

Is it that way ? Buckcleugh did say,
Lord Scroup must understand,
That he has not only done me wrong,
But my soveraign James of Scotland:
My Soveraign Lord King of Scotland
Thinks not his cousin Queen,
Will offer to invade his land,
Without leave asked and given ;
Thou stole into my master's land,
Which is within my conmand,
And in a plund'ring hostile way,
I'le let thee understand ;
Before day-light came thou stole a man,
And like a thief thou run away ;
This letter came to Lord Scroup's hand,
Which from Buckcleugh was sent,
Charging him then to release Kinment.
Or else he should repent ;
Scotland is not a fitting part,
I suppose England is the same ;
But if thou carry a valiant heart, I'le fight thee in Holland ;
There thou and I may both be free, which of us wins the day,
And be no cause of mutiny, nor invasions prey ;
Our Princes rare will not compare for dignity and fame,
It nothing doth transgress their laws what we do in Holland:
This message by a drummer sent,
To the Governour Lord Scroup,
A frivolous answer he returned,
Which made bold Buckcleugh to doubt ;
That he must into Carlisle ride,
And fetch the Kinment out,
The Armstrong was a hardy name
Into their own country ;
But like Clim of the Cleugh and little John,
On England they did prey,

Kinment's

Kinment's sirname was Armstroug,
He from Giltknocky sprang;
But Mengertoun he was the chief
Of the name of Armstrong,
It was not for their own respects,
That Buckcleugh turned their guardian;
It was for the honour of Scotland,
By reason he was Lord Warden;
He storm'd that any should presume
To enter the Scots border,
Either Cornish, Irish, English, Welch,
Unless they had his order;
If he had known when Lord Scroup did appear,
To enter the Scots ground, he had call'd up his rear;
But since he mist him in all Scotland's bounds,
In England he gave him sowre pears for plums.

Here follows how the Lord Buckcleugh *affronts the* Lord Scroup, *first by letters, and then by taking him prisoner out of the castle of Carlisle by Stratagem.*

THUS being vext, he shew the friends of the name,
   How the Lord Scroup had Willy Kinment tane;
And said, if they would but take part with him,
He knew a way to bring him back again;
To which demand they presently did conclude,
They would serve his honour to the last drop of their blood:
For certainty did prov'd to be a truth,
He'll still be call'd the good Lord of Buckcleugh;
His friend's advice that he desired to know,
Was Hawpasly, Thirlstone, Bonitown, and Tushilaw,
And Gaudilands his uncle's son,
With Whiteslade, Headshaw, and Sinton,
                                              And

And Gilbert Elliot he was not of his name,
But was his Honour's cousin-german ;
Those gentlemen in vote did all agree,
Five hundred to march in his Honour's company ;
He thank'd them for their vote, and said, that must not be,
Pick me out chosen men, no more but thirty three ;
At Thirlston his brethren they did begin,
They being the first cousin-german,
Both Walter and William was there in brief,
And presented their service unto their chief ;
Then Tushilaw did follow them,
And sent his two sons James and John,
With Mr Arthur Scot of Newburgh,
And Robert Scot of Gilmarscleugh,
Bowill his Brother William did thither come,
And John Scot brother to Bonnitoun ;
So did William of Haining, a valiant squire,
And William Scot of Hartwoodmire,
And William of Midgab came theretill,
He was grandsir to this laird of Horslyhill ;
Walter of Diphope a mettal man,
And John of Middlestead together came ;
Robert of Huntly he did not fail,
He came with the Scots of the water of Ail ;
So did Walter of Todrig that well could ride,
And Robert Scot brother to Whitslade,
Andrew of Sallinside he was one,
With James of Kirkhouse, and Askirks John ;
Robert of Headshaw himself would gang,
He was his Honour's cousin-german ;
Sinton and Wall, they stay'd at home,
Kirkhouse and Askirk went in their room ;
Because it was my Lord's decree,
But younger brethren they all should be ;

Some stout and valiant able men,
They would not stay at home,
And some related to my Lord they needs would go along,
Although my Lord to friends had letten't fall,
He would not have a landed man at all;
Yet valiant men they would not bide,
As appear'd by Hardin, Stobs, and Commonside;
They counted not their lives and lands so dear,
As the loss of the least title of their chief's honour.
But now I come for to explain,
The rest of these three and thirty men;
Satchells and Burnfoot they cross'd these strands
With Burnfoot in Tiviot and Gaudilands,
Hardin and Stobs before I did name,
Now follows Howfoord and Robertoun,
Howpasly he sent out his brother,
And Allan Haugh sent out another;
Clack and Alton did both accord,
To present their service unto my Lord;
Hassenden came without a call,
The antientest house among them all.
Thus I have gone through with pain,
To reckon the three and thirty men;
These gentlemen were all Scots,
Except Gilbert Elliot of the Stobs,
Which was a valiant gentleman,
And, as said before, my Lord's cousin-german;
These gentlemen did all conveen,
At Branksome-gate his Honour to attend;
They neither knew the cause, nor what the cause might be,
Before they came the length of Netherbie;
Although his Honour's trusty friend did ken,
Both some that went with him, and some that stay'd at home;

They

They had it on parol under great secrecy,
And to reveal't was worse than infamy;
When it pleas'd my Lord to ride, no man did know,
What his intention was, and whether he did go;
Except his counsellors, knights and gentlemen of fame,
Which passed not above seven or eight in all the name;
Wherever he went, he had one or two of them,
And for the rest he let them nothing ken.
  But now for to proceeed without delay,
Buckcleugh from Branksom took the way,
Through the woods of Esk in a full carrier went he,
To the Woodhouslies which is near to Netherbie;
And there a while continued he,
He brought wrights along in his company;
And caused them scaling-ladders make,
Although the wrights knew not for what;
Both artificial, long and strong,
There was six horsemen to carry them along;
In a high carrier my Lord did ride,
To the Woodhouslies on the border side;
For Netherbie is in English ground,
But the Woodhouslies is in Scotland;
There is a long mile them between,
Divided by the river of Esk her furious streams;
My Lord caused raise a vulgar report,
That he was only come to hold a justice-court:
Which caused fugitives to flie,
Unto the woods and mountains high;
And for the ladders tight and tall,
Was made for the towers of Branksom-hall;
Though it was made long and strong and most compleat,
To reach Carlisle's castle's battlement;
Such excuses there was for every thing,
But for's Honour's intention there was no din:

Most privately he his course did steer,
About Christmas, the hinder end of the year:
The day was past before the wrights had done,
Then it was long eight mile to Carlisle town,
The way was deep, and the water so strong,
' And the ladder was fifty foot long;
The firmament was dark, the gods was not in place,
Them Madam Night did show her ebon'd face;
Luna in sable mantel her course did steer,
And Jupiter he no way did appear;
Then scorching Sol, he was gone to his rest
And Titan had tane lodging in the west;
Saturn he did rule into that strain,
Mars and Venus under cloud remain'd;
Jove's thunder-bolts in skies did not appear,
Juno mask'd in fog, the night was no ways clear;
But yet his Honour he did no longer bide,
But paced throughout the muir to the river Eden-side;
Near the Stonish-bank my Lord a time did stay,
And left the one half of his company,
For fear they had made noise or din,
Near the castle they should come,
The river was in no great rage,
They cross'd near half a mile below the bridge;
Then along the sands with no noise at all,
They come close under the castle wall;
Then mask'd Midnight slowth did keep,
And mortal eyes was inclin'd to sleep;
Immediately they did their ladder plant,
Which reach'd the castle's battlement;
Then up the ladder they reer but doubt,
And broke a sheet of leid on the castle top,
A passage made, and in they came,
The Cape-house door they burst in twain;
Then down the stairs they come amain,
Where Kinmont fetter'd lay within.

          Then

Then with fore-hammers doors they broke down,
Amazing the Lord Scroup, and all his garrison;
They hors'd Kinment with his bolts upon a strong man's back,
And to the castle top in the ladder they did him set,
The Warden's trumpets did most sweetly sound,
Which put the garrison in a fear,
That all Scotland was come;
The Governour thought the castle had been gone,
He intended for to run and surely to save none;
Then Kinment said, when first here I did come,
Lord Scroup engaged me to take leave of him;
Then with a turning voice he did cry out;
Farewell, farewell, to my good Lord Scroup,
Which terrified the English more,
By an hundred times than they were before;
Then down the ladder in haste they Willy gat,
And set him sadle-aside upon a horse's back.
Mean time the trumpets sounded, Come if ye dare,
' They were the last men that came down the wooden stair,
They mounted all with speed, and safely did return
The self same way they formerly did come;
They observ'd neither file nor rank,
They met with the rest of the party at Stenick's bank;
Carlisle's dark muirs they did pass through,
There was never a man did them pursue,
To Line's water they come with speed,
Then past the muirs on the other side;
Then Kinment Willy cry'd out with pain,
And said his irons had him undone,
The which to his legs stuck like burs,
· He never before rode with such large spurs;
They stay'd for no smith on the English ground,
At Canninbie they arrived into Scotland:
Without loss or hurt to any man.
· At Canninbie a smith they faud;

By that time Aurora did appear,
Then bright Phœbus spread her beams most clear;
The smith on haste was set to work,
' And fyl'd the irons off Willy Kinment;
Yet Kinment Willie durst not stay at home,
But to Branksome place, he with his Honour came.
   The Lord Scroup afrighted, he did to London hie,
' And to Elizabeth his queen, he form'd many a lie;
And that how King James the sixth of Scotland then
Sent to assault her castle with an host of men:
Which put her garrison in a terrible fear,
And the villain Kinment Willy carried away clear;
Such numbers broke in at the castle top,
And brought Kinment Willy out of the pit:
He told the queen he thought to flee in haste,
The city could not stand, the castle being lost,
The vulgar being amazed in such a sort,
It was bright day or he durst open the port:
They had left the ladder standing at the wall:
But in haste they were returned to Scotland all:
Wherefore in sign and token of my loyalty,
I here complain of Scotland's villany,
And especially of that desperat youth,
The Scots warden, he's call'd, lord of Buckcleugh:
The queen caused her council to conveen,
And shew them how Carlisle's garrison,
Late by the Scots she was affronted,
For they on her castle were high mounted:
And broke in at the very top,
And reliev'd Kinment from the pit,
The Queen and her council did command,
A messenger to pass into Scotland,
To ask King James what was his reason,
In a hostile way to assault the garrison

With

With such an host of men of war,
And fetcht away her prisoner:
The King the message soon did understand,
And shew his cusin the Queen of England,
He then desired her Majesty,
She would be pleased and satisfied,
And understand how things are come and gone,
Which of the nations had done other wrong:
To make herself the judge, he was content,
And according to their merits she should give out judgement:
For on his royal word he did explain,
Scroup was first faulter to the Scots nation:
Lord Scroup he did begin to that effect,
To invade our land, and imprison our subjects:
With three hundred horse to come into our land,
Without leave of our warden, or any of our command:
A very insolent act against our crown and dignity,
By the law of arms, he doth deserve to die:
Our stout lord warden not being in place,
Though Scroup much wrong'd our nation, and did him disgrace;
It seems he did appeal him privately to fight,
But like a coward he did his challenge slight:
And so without our order, he went out,
To be reveng'd upon the base Lord Scroup:
No more but sixteen men to Carlisle came,
And gave alarm to castle and the town,
Wherein a thousand did remain,
Your Majesty may think he was a stout captain;
Our prisoner he did but relieve again,
And none of your subjects either hurt or slain:
We think his valour merits some reward,
That of your towers and castles no way was afraid;
We think your governour deserves both lack and shame,
That suffered sixteen men your prisoner to gain:

That

That governour is not a souldier stout,
Who being a thousand strong, and durst not venture out:
With letters to such purpose the messenger did return,
And expressly shew the Queen, she being at London;
Her council did conveen, and the decree gave out,
' That Scroup was all the blame of the passage went about:
The English council call'd Buckcleugh a man compleat,
' Which did merit honour, he must be of a heroic spirit:
Both King and council sounded his commendation,
Wishing for many such within their English nation:
Such praises made the Queen her royal Majesty
Be most desirous that bold Buckcleugh to see.
The Queen wrote to King James,
All the whole and sole truth,
With a fervent desire to see the lord Buckcleugh.
The King sent for Buckcleugh, and to him did unfold,
Shewing him, he must go see
His cusin, Queen of England:
Buckcleugh did yeeld to venture life and land,
And do whatever the King did him command:
A certain time the King did him confer,
And shew he was a free man, and no prisoner;
You with your servants had best go there by land,
For all you have to do, it's to kiss our cusin's hand:
The fixed day when that my Lord should go,
Was in the month of March, when husbandmen corn sow;
A rumor rose, and spread through the whole country,
How the Lord Buckcleugh he must at London die;
Uupon the fixed day his Honour went,
Which caused many hundreds to lament,
Which said alas! they were undone,
And fear'd my Lord should ne're return again;
The whold name of *Scot*, and all his friends about,
Maxwel and Johnston conveyed him out;
The Humes came from the Merss.

            And

Aud in Ednem-Haugh did bide;
A thousand Gentlemen conveyed him over Tweed;
They put him to Flowden field,
The length of Scotland's ground;
And there took leave, and back again return'd;
Toward London rode, they did themselves apply,
Thirlston, Sir Robert Scot bear his Honour company;
No more there past with his Honor along,
But three domestick servants, and Sir Robert Scot had one:
The day being Tuesday, twenty four mile they wan,
And lodged in Morpeth, into Northumberland;
On Wedensday twenty four miles they came,
Into the principality of Durham;
On Thursday they their course did steer,
Thirty four miles to Borrow-bridge in York-shire;
On Friday to Duncaster his Honor hade;
Twenty eight mile that day he no less rade:
To view the town his Honor did desire,
It being within the county of York-shire;
For as men pass along the road,
York-shire is sixty six miles broad;
On Saturday, twenty eight mile he went,
To New-wark town that stands upon Trent,
And all the Sabbath his Honor did remain,
The town lies in the county of Notingham;
On Munday he his course did steer,
Twenty six miles to Stenfoord in Lincoln-shire;
On Tuesday twenty short mile he came,
To the town and shire called Huntingtoun;
On Wednesday his Honor did fare,
Twenty nine miles to Ware in Hartford-shire;
On Thursday he did go betwixt,
Ware and Troynovent in Middlesex,
Troynovent was the antient name;

King Lud brought it to be call'd London.
He did not sooner London gain,
Till it was noised among the English-men,
They run in flocks, and did on's Honor gaze,
As he had been the monster slain by Hercules,
The people to their neighbours did cry out,
Come let us go, and see that valiant Scot:
Which out of Carlisle stoutly took,
Kinment in spight of our Lord Scroup,
In Carlisle Kinment did remain,
Whilst this Scot fetcht him out, and had but sixteen men,
At London Kinment Willy his name was better known,
Nor it was in the Border-side where his fore-fathers were born:
But now for to conclude within a little time,
The good Lord of Buckcleugh to the English court did win;
That valiant cavalier he came with such a grace,
The English wardens usher'd him to the presence;
Notice came to the Queen, that bold Buckcleugh was there,
Then she left her private chamber, and in presence did appear;
The Queen in modesty, a complement did frame,
Desiring to know the health of his master,
Her cousin good King James,
A sign of war to me appears, and makes great variance;
Amongst such blades who do invade,
And become league-breakers,
Since ye intrude within our border,
And did assault our garison,
And Kinment reliev'd without order;
Ye make but a scar-crow of England's Queen,
I thought my cusin James yet King,
Should never done his friend such wrong,
But this I leave to another time;
He may repent or it be long.

Buckcleugh's

Buckcleugh's Speech.

THEN bold Buckcleugh spoke forth the truth;
And to the Queen he did declare:
His master Scotland's King was free of every thing,
It is your Majesty that makes all the jars;
Your Majesty did order give,
As it appears the Lord Scroup lately said,
That with three hundred horse he would march north,
My master's kingdom to invade;
And took his subjects there captive.
This will appear to be a wrong,
And in Carlisle keept him in bondage,
Where he laid him into fetters strong,
Whilst I have life, or any strength:
I'le fight for my master's dignity,
His captive subjects to relieve,
By truth it shall not fail in me:
My Royal Master, and dread Soveraign,
I am his Majestie's subject born,
And to none other prince but he,
To the oath of alledgeance I'le be sworn:
Wherever his subjects are prisoners tane,
If I can relieve them, they shall not remain.
I never thought of such a lawless act,
To invade your nation, and your subjects take:
If I had done, your Majesty had storm'd,
But unlawful tane, unlawful he return'd,
When any of your subjects unlawfully broke out,
I never did intrude like your governour Lord Scroup,
But to your wardens I did still complain,
Who sent me his malefactor, I sent him mine again.

The Queen's Answer.

THE Queen she lent attentive ear,
    And of his Honour's courage she did much admire,
My Lord, she said, your speech I'll keep in mind,
And answer you at some other time;
But neither at court, nor council ye shall appear,
For I conceive you're a resolute cavalier:
At Channel-hall your lodging shall be there,
Then through our privy-garden to court ye may repair,
For your disport when to the court ye come,
Peruse our library, either even or morn,
At your own pleasure what time so e're it be,
And for your clearer passage ye shall have a private key,
Except our counsellors and officers in charge,
We do not grant to any, but your merits to deserve;
Thrice worthy Lord, your merits do proclaim,
How honour's noble mark is still your aim;
And to attain the which thou holds thy hands to study,
That thy deserts by fame has won thee gain already,
Industrious loyalty doth use, and all men tell,
To aim at honour it levels very well,
And in your trusty service shot compleat,
That in the end he's sure have hit the white;
Let fortune frown or smile ye are content,
At all assays to bear a heart true bent,
Though sin and hell work mortals to betray,
Against their malice God hath arm'd thy way:
When life and land and all away is fled,
Yet thy noble actions is much honoured,
Thy loyal service to thy King doth prove,
That to thy country thy heart is join'd in love;
Love is a dying life, a living death,
A vapour, shadow, a bubble, and a breath;

An idle babble, and a poultrey toy,
Whose greatest pattern is a blinded boy,
When fortune, love and death their task hath done,
Fame makes our life through many ages run ;
For be our actions good or ill,
Fame keeps a record of our doings still :
By fame great Julius Caesar ever lives,
And fame infamous life to Nero gives :
Those that 'scapes fortune and extreams of love,
Unto their longest homes by death are driven.
When Caesar, Kesar subjects, objects most,
Be all alike consum'd to dirt and dust,
Death endeth all our cares, or cares increase,
It sends us into lasting pain or bless.

 Awake, awake my muse, thou sleeps too long,
To bold Buckcleugh again I will return,
Expressing of the time that he did there resort,
And his entertainment at the English court,
For banquets, he had store, and that most free,
Each day by some of their nobility ;
His attendance was by nobles there,
As he had been a prince late come from afar ;
The north-country English could not be at rest,
While the Scots warden came to be their guest.
Six weeks at court continued he,
Still feasted with their nobility ;
To the Queen's majesty he made redress,
When she would be pleased he should go from hence
The Queen was mute, and let the question slide,
Yet wished that he might there abide ;
But yet the King of Scots she had no mind to wrong,
By reason that he was her royal dear cousin,
To whom she hop'd to prove as kind,
As mother might do, to please his mind ;

What misses are past, we do declare,
Your King our cousin will us repair,
Your master our cousin and we will agree,
We have already acquainted his majesty;
But, my Lord, if you will here remain,
Or if you will return again,
At your master's hands we'll get you free,
' And here you shall have a sallary.
He humbly thank'd her majesty,
Showing the Queen that could not be,
For he had service in Holland,
And was bound to obey his master's command;
It was two much to be bound to three,
So beg'd that he might pardon'd be.
The Queen answer'd, my Lord, since it is so,
Ye shall be dispatch'd within a day or two,
And a letter ye shall carry along with thee
To our cousin of Scotland's majestie,
Wherein your heroic spirit we must commend,
And intend hereafter to be your friend;
Next day she call'd her secretar,
And charg'd him a letter to prepare,
To his majesty's King of Scotland,
Wherein she lets him understand,
She had past from her former wrong,
By reason Buckcleugh was a valiant man.
Ceasar and Tammerlan are valiant men, that's plain,
But in their own person they ventured not like him;
Regulus and Schipio was short of him against their foe,
Most stout Buckcleugh with his small train,
Scal'd a castle, and had but sixteen men,
And brought a prisoner with him along,
That was bound in chains and irons most strong,

Mounts to the castle top so high,
And cliverly brought him away:
Yet a thousand men there was within,
Of horse and foot in the garison,
Although it did us much offend,
Yet his courage we must commend;
The Queen to him the letter gave,
And pleasantly she took her leave,
Wishing him a good journey home,
In hopes no more her castle he'd storm.
Now I not intend for to set down,
How that his Honour returned home;
But James the Sixth that gracious King,
Was well content of his home coming.

Now follows the Antiquity of the Name of Scot.

SINCE from all danger Buckcleugh was free,
I must speak something of his familie,
That Lord Buckcleugh his fame spread far,
Call'd Walter Lord Scot of Whitchester;
' Some late start-up brau-new gentlemen,
' That hardly knows from whence their fathers came,
Except from red nos'd Robin,
Or Trail Wallet, countrey Tom,
' The sons of Cannongate Bess,
' That well could play her game;
Whose labouring heads as great as any house,
These calumnizing fellows can stagger stare and shame,
And swear the name of Scot is but a new com'd name,
These new cornuted gentlemen, why should they lie,
' Mr George Buchannan and Hector Boetius can let them see,
A thousand years, if I do not forget,
By chronicles I'le prove the name of Scot,

In King Achaius time that worthy prince,
John and Clement Scots they went to France,
In Paris they at first began,
In Charles the Great his time,
To instruct the Christian religion,
And there a colledge they did frame,
Which doth remain unto this very time;
And he that doth not believe me,
' Must read Buchannan, and he shall see ;
Some other authors I could give in,
But these are sufficient to them that's not blind;
Some says, they were not Scots to their name,
But only Scots by nation,
Yet Monks of Melross they were known,
Which then was in the Picts kingdom.
John Earl of Channerth sirnamed Scot,
To die without succession was his unfortunate lot :
Brave Alexander the first, a King both stout and good,
John Earl of Channerth married with his royal blood.
Before Alexander the first his brother Edgar did reign,
The first that was anoiuted of Scotland King;
Reverend John Scot he did surmount,
Who was Bishop Dumblane, and did the King anoint :
Mr Michael Scot that read the epistle at Rome,
He was in King Alexander the second's reign,
Thomas Lermont was first his man,
That was called the Rymer ever since then ;
And if my author doeth speak truth,
Mr Michael was descended from Buckcleugh ;
And if my author ye would know,
Bishop Spotswood's book these Scots do show :
How can these randy liars then,
Make the Scots to be a start-up clan,
Sure new start-ups themselves must be,
For ancient families scorn to lie :

But

But for the antiquity of the *Scot*,
There's one thing I have almost forgot,
Which is not worthy of nomination,
Yet to mark antiquity, I'le make relation;
In the second session of King David's parliament,
There was a statute made, which is yet extant,
That no man should presume to buy or sell,
With Highland men or *Scots* of Ewsdale;
Yet Ewsdale was not near the forrest,
Where brave Buckcleugh did dwell,
According to the old proverb,
They but fell from the Wain's tail,
But when these *Scots* did bear that stile,
King David resided in Carlisle,
Without and infang they disturb'd his court,
Which caus'd the King that act set out:
Here I speak nought but truth, all men may note,
The very true antiquity of the name of Scot,
And now my versing muse craves some repose,
' And while she sleeps, I'll spout a little prose.

KENNETH the second King of Scots, son to King Alpin, who was son to brave King Achaius forsaid, who made the league with Charles the Great Emperor of Germany, and King of France, the year seven hundred eighty seven; this King Kenneth called the Great, conquered the kingdom of the Picts, about the year of grace eight hundred and thirty nine, and join'd the kingdom of Picts unto the antient nation of Scotland. This victorious King Kenneth the second dyed in the twenty year of his reign: The Kingdom not being well settled in obedience to the crown, his brother Donald the fifth succeeded him, a very infamous King, and a great tyrant; he lost all Scotland to Striviling-bridge, by the Brittans and Saxons, the which time the King Osbridge, conquered great lands in Scotland, assisted by the Brittans; so

H that

that Striviling-bridge was made marches betwixt Scots, Brittans, and Englishmen. King Osbridge coined money in the castle of Striviling, by that the Starling money had first beginning, and died in the fifth year of his reign. King Constantin the second, the Conqueror's son, a valiant King, in whose time Heger and Hoba, with a great fleet of Danes landing in Fife, used great cruelty. King Constantin the second came with a great army against Hoba, and vanquished him; the Scots being proud of that victory, and neglecting themselves, there followed a cruel and desperat battle; at last the Scots were vanquished, and King Constantin with his nobles, and ten thousand of his army, killed in the fifteen year of his reign: Ethus, sirnamed the Swift, succeeded his father King Constantin; he died in the second year of his reign: Gregorius Magnus, Dongallus son, a worthy, stout, and valiant King, he freed Scotland all again from Osbridge, Saxons, and Englishmen; and enlarged his empire to the county and shire of Northumberland, Westmurland, and Cumberland; and confederat with Eleward King of Brittans, and after went to Ireland, and vanquished Braenus and Cornelius, after besieged Dublin, wherein was their young King Duncan, to whom he was made protector, during the King's minority; then returned to Scotland with a victorious army, and brought threescore pledges of the Irish nobility and gentry, under the age of thirty years; he died in the eighteen year of his reign. Donald the sixth was son to Constantin the second, a good, religious, valiant King; he succeeded King Gregory; in his time the Murrays and Rosses invading each other, with cruel killing, two thousand were killed in either parties; the King came upon them with a great army, and punished the principal of this rebellion to the death; he died in the eleventh year of his reign. Constantin the third, Ethus' son, succeeded him, a valiant prince, not fortunate in wars, he being vexed with war in the time of King Edward, surnamed Sinar, of the Saxons kind, and Edlston his bastard son; he became a Canon in St. Andrew's, and died in the forty year of his reign: Malcolm the first, Donald the sixth's son, a valiant prince, and a good justitiar; in his time, a confederacy was made, that Cumberland and Westmurland should be annexed to the kingdom of Scotland, and should be perpetually holden

by

by the prince of Scotland of fee, from the king of England, by virtue whereof, Indolphus, son to Constantin the third prince of Scotland, took possession in both Cumberland and Westmurland: The King died the ninth year of his reign. Indolphus, Constantin the third's son, succeeded King Malcolm the first, a noble, valiant prince; he vanquished Athagen prince of Norway, and Theodorick prince of Denmark; he died in the ninth year of his reign: Duffus, Malcolm the first's son, succeeded King Indolphus, a good prince, and a severe justitiar; he died in the fifth year of his reign; Colonus, Indolphus son, succeeded King Duffus; He died in the fourth year of his reign. Kenneth the third, son to Malcolm the first, a brave King, and a good justitiar; from the death of Kenneth the second, which conquered the Picts, to the reign of Kenneth the third, we had nine Kings in Scotland: I have set down particularly how long every King's reign was, *in cumulo* they reigned a hundred and nine years, most of them, although I have not expressed, they were most of them killed in the field, being so possest with war on every side, what by Denmark and Norway on the one side, the Brittans and Saxons on the other side, poor little Scotland had much to do to get her feet holden among them: For in all that time of an hundred and nine years, there was but one victorious conquering prince, which was King Gregory: So that the borders in these lands in England aforesaid, being sometimes under the command of the Scots, and sometimes of the English, they became so rude and insolent, that they would never be governed before Kenneth the third brought them under obedience to the crown of Scotland; yet they were never under sole obedience till the reign of Malcolm the third, surnamed Canmor; he dispatch'd them all, and gave their lands and inheritance to others, which were loyal subjects.

AND now with sleep my muse hath eas'd her brain,
I'le turn my stile to rhyming verse again;
King Kenneth the second, that prince of high renown,
He vanquish'd the Picts, and conquer'd their crown,
In revenge of his father's death, which basely they murther'd

For which victorious Kenneth mow'd them down,
And annexed their realm under Scotland's crown;
The year of grace he did their crown annex,
Was in the eight hundred and thirty six,
Or in the fourty six, I know not whether,
The Kingdoms they were joyn'd together,
Being the fourth or fourteenth year of his reign;
And ere the twentieth he did return,
To his mother earth, from whence he came;
His soul and hope doth reach the sky,
His fame to Titans rise did fly.
Donald the fifth succeeded his brother then,
And lost as much as King Kenneth won,
A vitious, odious King, he play'd at swig,
Whilst he lost Scotland all to Striviling-bridge,
Yet at's beginning he did come speed,
And vanquish'd his enemies on the South-side Tweed;
The Picts that fled among the English-men,
Requested Osbridge and Ella, two great princes of England,
To move war against their enemies in Scotland,
Both English, Brittans, Picts, these princes brought,
Which Donald vanquish'd at Jedburgh,
He was so insolent after his victory,
To the river of Tweed he came with his army,
And two ships he took with wine and victuals rare,
And order'd every souldier for to have their share.
King Donald was given to variosity and greed,
With lust of body, he could ne're be satisfied,
The whole camp they had their paramours,
And was full of taverns, of bordels, and whoors;
They followed carding, dyeing, and contentious trouble,
That each of them, they did kill one another.
King Osbridge having advertisement anone,
Rais'd a new army, and to the Scots he came;

And

And kill'd twenty thousand men compleat,
' Without armour, and all fast asleep.
That vile King was tane, as has been said,
And in derision through his countrey led ;
At which time King Osbridge conquer'd much land,
And that the south parts of Scotland fand,
Assisted by the Brittans, so that he,
Caus'd Stirling-bridge the marches for to be ;
For Saxons, Brittans and English-men,
In three Kings reigns they kept that garrison,
In Stirling castle Osbridge did money coyn ;
From which the Sterling money had it's first name ;
The Scots valu'd not the laud did belong to the Pict.
But the lands of Albion Osbridge did afflict ;
Ther's Galloway, and the isle of Man,
Was lands of Scotland since the first King Fergus came.
So was Kyle and Carrick, all in haill,
Arron through Lennox, with the Nether-ward of Clidsdail ;
The Mers and Tiviot-dail was Picts lands,
And so was all the three Louthians,
So was Peebles, Selkirk, and Over-ward of Clidsdail ;
Nithsdail, and Annandail ; with the five kirks of Eskdail,
' Drunken Donald all these lands did tyne,
But Gregorius Magnus recover'd them again,
From Gregorie's death, to Kenneth the third's reign,
The borders obey'd neither God, nor King ;
Kenneth the third lov'd deer, both red and fallow,
' Above all princes since King Dornadilla :
Hunting was the sport he liked best,
For all our south-parts was wood and forrest,
Except here and there a summering plain,
Into which his keepers did remain.

MY muse has been astray a certain time,
But now in case for to return again;
With the name of Scot she's minded to contain,
Because they are her worthy noble friends,
The year of grace sixteen hundred and twenty nine,
Carlaverock was a garrison in that time,
Collonel Monro a German souldier he,
Blockt up the castle both by land and sea,
Into that leigure I did remain,
In Cockburn's company, I was a souldier then;
And my chance was with my command to pass,
To the English side call'd Burgh under Bowness.
By fortune I fell in a gentleman's companie,
Call'd Lancelot Scot, who was most kind to me;
He shew'd me his ancestors hail,
Did live into that spot;
Since Carlisle walls were re-built,
By David King of Scots;
A book he gave to me, call'd Mr Michael's creed,
' But never a word at that time I could read,
What he read to me, I have it not forgot:
It was th' original of our south countrey-Scots.
He said, that book which he gave me,
Was of Mr Michael Scot's historie,
Which history was never yet read through.
' Nor never will, for no man dare it do;
Young scholars have pickt out some thing,
From the contents, that dare not read within.
He carried me along into the castle then,
And shew his written book hanging on an iron pin:
His writing pen did seem to me to be
Of harden'd mettal, like steil, or accumie;
The volume of it did seem so large to me,

As

As the book of martyrs and Turks historie;
Then in the church he let me see,
A stone where Mr Michael Scot did lie.
I ask'd at him how that could appear,
Mr Michael had been dead above five hundred year;
He shew'd me none durst bury under that stone,
More than he had been dead few years agone,
For Mr Michael's name does terrifie each one,
That vulgar people dare scarce look on the stone,
And more it us'd to pay the Saxons a fee,
For strangers are desirous that stone to see;
That Lancelot Scot he wearied not,
To shew me every thing,
' And then incontinent to the ale-house did return,
' Where we had the other cup and the other can,
There was no cause of feed,
Lancelot he said, I was not a gentleman,
That was not bred to read;
But to proceed, he wearied not,
To shew the original of the border Scot.
He said, that book did let him understand,
How the Scots of Buckcleugh gain'd both name and land;
He said, gentlemen in Galloway by fate,
Had fallen at odds, and a riot did commit;
For in these days, as he did say,
It was call'd Brigants that's now call'd Galloway.
Two valiant lads of these Brigants
Were censured to be gone,
Then to the south they took their way.
And arrived at Rankelburn,
At Rankelburn where they did come,
The keeper was call'd Brydine,
They humbly then did him intreat,
For meat, drink, and lodging;

The

The keeper stood and then did look.
And saw them pretty men,
Immediatly grants their request,
And to his house they came ;
To wind a horn they did not scorn,
In the loftiest degree,
Which made the Forrester conceive,
They were better keepers than he ;
In Ettrick-forrest, Megget's-head,
Meucra and Rankelburn-grain,
There was no keepers in the south,
That could compare with them ;
These Gentlemen were brethren born,
If histories be not amiss ;
The one of them called John Scot,
And the other of them called Wat English.

KING KENNETH then a hunting came,
To the Cacra-cross did resort,
And all the nobles of his court,
They hither came to see the sport ;
Of Ettrick's-hew he took a view,
Then to the left hand did turn,
Where he did see that forrest hie,
Which then was called Rankelburn ;
The keepers and the strouse-men came,
With shouts from hill to hill,
With hound and horn they rais'd the deer,
But little blood did spill ;
A buck did come that was so run.
Hard by the Cacra-cross,
He mean'd to be at Rankelburn,
Finding himself at loss :

The

The hill was steep, the bogs were deep,
With woods and heather strong,
By a mile of ground there none came near it,
But footmen that did run;
Then one of these two gentlemen
Which from Galloway did come,
Both hounds and deer he keeped near
To the water in Rankelburn:
And then the buck being spent and gone,
He on the hounds did turn,
That gentleman came first along,
And catch'd him by the horn,
Alive he cast him on his back,
Or any man came there,
And to the Cacra-cross did trot,
Against the hill a mile and mair;
The King saw him a pretty man,
And ask'd his name, from whence he came,
He said from Galloway he came,
If't please your Grace my name is John;
The deer being curied in that place
At his Majesty's demand,
Then John of Galloway ran apace
And fetch'd water to his hands;
The King did wash into a dish,
And Galloway John he wot,
He said thy name now after this,
Shall e're be call'd John Scot;
The forrest and the deer therein,
We commit to thy hand,
For thou shall sure the ranger be,
If thou obey command;
And for the buck thou stontly brought,
To us up that steep heugh,
Thy desiguation ever shall
Be John Scot in Buckscleugh.

By strength of limb and youthfull spring,
Fortune may favour still,
And if thou prove obedient,
We'll mend thee when we will;
John humbly then thanked the King,
And promis'd to be loyal,
And earnestly beg'd his Majesty,
That he would make a tryal;
My name is John, and I'm alone,
Into this strange country,
Except one brother with me came,
To bear me company;
What is his name then said the King?
He answer'd, his name is Wat;
Ye are very well met, then said the King,
He shall be English, and ye are Scot;
At Bellanden let him remain
Fast by the forrest side,
Where he may do us service too,
And assist you with his aid.
I do believe, as my author did declare,
How the original of Buckcleugh was a valiant forrester,
It's most like to be true which I have plainly shown,
The old families of Buckcleugh did carry a hunting-horn
Buckcleugh, if that my author doth speak truth,
It's long since he began,
In the third King Kenneth's reign,
He to the forrest came.
The first of their genealogy,
Though chronicles be rent and torn,
And made their ends upon the sea;
Of late into the Usurper's time,
Our registers away were tane,
Many of them perish'd in the main,
And never came ashore again.

In Queen Mary's reign they had bad handling,
Sometimes fortune favour'd, and sometimes frown'd,
'Twixt stools, if men do miss their mark,
Then their bottom sure goes to the ground.
In Edward Longshank's time, King of England,
Our monuments were lost and gone,
Our chronicles and registers to London went,
Yet not returned again.
In the reign of the third Constantine,
All substance from this land was tane,
By that Saxon King Edward sirnamed Cinar,
And Edleston his bastard son;
Since these hurli-burlies tops-a-turvies,
So oft this land they have undone,
That a native durst not show himself,
Except on the tops of the mountains;
When our records were sent away,
The vulgar sort they were not free,
Therefore there was particular acts,
For to be cloaks to their knavery;
The chronicle may err, some men may be preferr'd,
In every science there is some cheatry;
For if an inferior man to a clerk shall come,
And possess him of such gallantry,
Then he'll take a word alone,
And so reward him with his coin,
Which will cause the clerk blaze him to the sky,
Within two hundred year may be it do appear,
If the world shall stand so long,
That the late made Purves act,
Which he obtained to cover his fact,
Will raise his needy friends to be gentlemen;
That bold Buckcleugh was none of them.

That

That ever bought his honour with coin ;
His valour did it gain, in Holland and in Swain,
And against the Saxon's seed they oft did honour gain.
From the family of Buckcleugh,
There has sprung many a man,
Four hundred years ago ;
Hassinden he was one,
Descended of that line, and still he doth remain,
And evident's speaks truth, the same the truth proclaims.
Though chronicles be lost from many a family,
These characters that remains, the truth they let us see,
Sir Alexander Scot of Hassinden was knight,
With good King James the Fourth, he was killed at Flowdon fight.
From Hassinden did spring before that time
The families of Wall, Delorian, and Haining,
The south-country gentry is known for truth,
Was exercised in arms into their youth,
None other education they did apply,
But Jack and spear against their enemy ;
And because it was their daily exercise,
' They never sought to be chronicliz'd :
But when a courtier did any valiant fate,
He was cry'd up to th' stars, and made Lord of State.
But now advance my muse, and declare the truth,
Of brave John Scot the original of Buckcleugh ;
' And because thou art weary, as I suppose,
' I'll refrain verse, and turn myself to prose ;
Good Lancelot Scot, I think his book be true,
Old Rankelburn is design'd Buckcleugh now ;
Yet in his book no Balls read he,
It was Buckscleugh they read to me ;
He told me the name, the place, the coat,
Came all by the hunting of the buck :

In Scotland no Buckcleugh was then,
Before the Buck in the Cleugh was slain;
Nights-men at first they did appear,
Because moon and stars to their arms they bear,
Their crest, supporters, and hunting-horn,
Showes their beginning from hunting came;
Their name and stile the book did say,
John gain'd them both into one day:
The very place where that the buck was slain,
He built a stone house, and there he did remain;
He built a church into that forrest hie,
There was no man to come to it, but his own family;
The house's ground-work yet is to be seen;
And at that church, I many times have been,
A burial place it yet keeps out,
For any poor folk that lyes round about;
To the paroch church it's long six mile,
Therefore they bury yet to save travel;
My Guid-sir Satchels, I heard him declare,
There was nine Lairds of Buckcleugh buried there;
But now with rubish and earth it's fill'd up so high,
That no man can the through-stones see,
But nine tomb-stones he saw with both his eyne,
' But knew not who was buried under them;
Also they built a miln on that same burn,
To grind dogs-bran, though there there grew no corn,
For in my own time corn little there hath been,
There was neither rig nor fur for to be seen,
But hills and mountains on every side,
The haugh below, scarce a hundred foot wide;
Yet there's a miln-steed in that brook,
And the church-walls I have seen them all up,
It is two reasonable myle
Between the miln-steed and the kirk-style;

My Guid-sir told me there he had seen,
A holy cross, and a font-stone;
The paroch being twenty mile about,
But hardly sixteen folks remain in it.
All the corn I have seen there in a year,
Was scarce the sowing of six firlots of bear;
And for neighbours to come with good will,
There was no corn to grind into that mill,
' If heather-tops had been meal of the best,
' Then Buckcleugh-mill had gotten a noble grist,
Now wearied muse to rest thou may resort,
' Whilst I a little prose report.

I Heard my Guid-sir tell, that he had heard all men say, the reason why the lairds of Buckcleugh did build that miln, was, for the use of their houses, for grinding of flour, meal, and malt, but especially bran for his dogs, and the corn came out of other barronies, which was then in his possession, as the Ewards in Tweddale, the barrony of Eckfoord, Grimslies in east-Tiviotdail, and other barronies, and lands under his command; this is spoken by tradition to this time. But sure if such things were, as it hath been by all appearance, it must be long after the beginning of the honourable family of Buckcleugh; for at that time, Buckcleugh must needs be a person of much honour and renown, and of a very competent estate, when he built a church and a miln in such a wild forrest as Rankelburn, now called Buckcleugh, where there was no people to come to the church, except his own family, nor girst to his miln, except what he caused to come for his own use, near twenty myle in each side of his own residence. My Guid-sir Satchells told me, that he was with Walter called the good Lord of Buckcleugh, after he came from the schools, and Robert of Thirlston, after Sir Robert, they being come from the colledge of St Andrew's, where they had been at learning, by reason King James the Sixth was of that university, my Lord and Sir Robert being of the King's age, in the year one thousand five hundred and sixty six, was desirous to pass their time
there;

there; and, at their return, the Lord Buckcleugh being ready to go to his travels, was curious to see these tomb-stones of his ancestors, which was in that kirk, in the forrest of Rankelburn; the most part of the wall was standing then, and the font-stone within the kirk, and a cross before the kirk-door; the rubbish and earth being casten out, and the stones clean swept, the Lord, and many of his friends came to see them, where they did discern one stone, which had the antient coat of arms on it; that is to say, two crests, and a mulet born on a counter-scarf, with a hunting-horn in the field, supported with a hart of grace and a hart of leice, alias a hound, and a buck, and a buck's head torn from the crest, which only seem to be from hunters and forresters. The other stones had drawn upon them like unto a hand and sword, and others of them had a sword and a lance all along the stone; Robert Scot said, that he believed, that it was four hundred years since the last of these stones had been laid, and it was near an hundred year since that time; I judge the Lord Buckcleugh was about twenty one, or twenty two years at that time, so it must needs be near to an hundred years since.

The lands of Buckcleugh they did possess,
Three hundred years ere they had writ or wax;
And since that time that they a right did rear,
'It's said to be from King Robert the Third, call'd John Fern-year.

Now follows the several places of residence of the family of Buckcleugh.

NOW my jocking muse assist my rhyme compleat,
I'm drown'd in prose since thou lay down to sleep;
Thy journey's long, and so thou must not stay,
'We'l take some part of Tweddale in our way;
The barrony of Eward was Buckcleugh's share,
And yet they are supperior
Over Eward and Neither Eward was in the barrony,
With Kirk-Eward, Lady Eward, and Lock Eward, all three;

These

These towns most sweet surround a pleasant hill,
And Scotstoun-hall doth join unto them still.
It was call'd Scotstoun-hall when Buckcleugh in it did dwell,
Unto this time it is call'd Scotstoun still:
It was in Kirk-Eward paroch then,
But now it's in the paroch of Lintoun;
There is three towers in it was mounted high,
And each of them had their own entry,
A sally-door did enter on,
Which serv'd all three, and no man kend,
When Buckcleugh at Scots-hall kept his house,
Then Peebles-church was his burial place,
In the cross-kirk there has buried been
Of the Lairds of Buckcleugh, either six or seven;
There can none say but it's two hundred year
Since any of them was buried there;
The Earls of Hamiltoun and Douglas,
To brave Buckcleugh shewed great kindness,
Their kindness with him did prevail,
That he must live near them in Clidsdail;
Scots-hall he left standing alone,
And went to live at Mordistoun;
And there a brave house he did rear,
Which to this time it doth appear;
Several ages after, he did these lands excamb,
With Inglis that was the Laird of Branksom;
And since that time I can mak't appear,
It's near two hundred and fifty year,
That familie they still were valiant men,
No Baron was better served into Britain,
The Barons of Buckcleugh they kept at their call,
Four and twenty gentlemen in their hall,
All being of his name and kin,
Each two had a servant to wait on them;

Before

Before supper and dinner most renown'd,
The bells rung and the trumpets sounded,
And more than that I do confess,
They kept four and twenty pensioners;
Think not I lie, or do me blame,
For the pensioners I can all name;
There's men alive elder than I,
They know if I speak truth or lie;
Ev'ry pensioner a room did gain,
For service done and to be done,
This I'le let the reader understand.
The name of both the men and land,
Which they posses'd it is of truth,
Both from the Lairds and Lords of Buckcleugh.
But now, my muse, I'le give it in thy chose,
' Stay or go sleep, for I must write in prose.

Now follows the gentlemens names that were pensioners to the house of Buckcleugh, *with the lands they possess'd for their service.*

WALTER SCOT of North-house, the first gentleman descended from the family, in a former age Robert Scot of Allanmouth; David Scot of Stobiscot, brother to Sir Walter Scot of Gaudilands; David Scot of Raes-know, one of the house of Allan-haugh; Robert Scot of Clack, the land of Fennick for his service; William Scot in Hawick, call'd William in the Mott, brother to Walter Scot of Hardin, possest these lands without the West-port for his service; John Scot of Monks-tower, brother to old William Scot of Altoun; Robert Scot of Easter-Groundiston, brother son to Robert Scot of Headshaw; James Scot of Altoun Crofts, Raes-know, and Allanmouth, were all of the family of Allanhaugh; Thomas Scot in Wester-Groundiston brother to William Scot of Whitehaugh, desended of the antient family of Buckcleugh; John Scot in Drinkston, descended of the antient family of Robert-toun; William Scot in Lies, alias Millma, called William Scot of Catslac-know, descended from the antient family of Dryhop: Robert Scot

Scot in Clarilaw descended from the antient house of Hassanden; William Scot of Totchahaugh, from the foresaid family of Bortoheugh; Andrew Scot of Totchahill from the family of Robertoun; John Scot in Stowslie;   Scot of Whames, descended from the North-house;
Scot of Castlehill, was of that kind; Walter Scot of Chappel-hill, he was half-brother to the Laird of Chisholm; Robert Scot of Howford had the lands of Cowd-house for his service; Robert Scot of Satchels had Southinrig for his service; Robert Scot of Langup had the land of Outter-huntly for his service, for several ages; there was one William Scot, commonly called Cut at the Black, he had the lands of Nether-Delorian for his service; Walter Gladstanes had Whitlaw. These twenty four were all of the name of Scot except Walter Gladstanes of Whitlaw, who was nearly related to my Lord; this William Scot of Delorian, commonly call'd Cut at the Black, he was a brother of the antient house of Haining, which house of Haining is descended from the antient house of Hassanden; and from the foresaid William Scot of Delorian, sprung the family of Scotstarbet and Elie, now called Ardross, their original being from Sir Alexander Scot of Hassanden; that valiant knight was kill'd with his prince King James the Fourth at Flowden field. Now I come to Sir Walter Scot of Buckcleugh, who was grand-father to Walter the good Lord of Buckcleugh. These twenty three pensioners, all of his own name of Scot, and Walter Gledstanes of Whitlaw, a near cousin of my Lord's, as aforesaid; they were ready on all occasions, when his Honour pleased cause to advertise them. It was known to many in the country better than it is to me, that the rents of these lands, which the Lairds and Lords of Buckcleugh did freely bestow upon their friends, will amount above twelve or fourteen thousand merks a year: This I have thought good to let the reader see the benefit which the younger brethren of the name had by their chief, when he was but a Baron and Knight, they were esteemed with more respect than they have been since; Sir William Scot of Branksom, who never survived to be Laird or Lord of Buckcleugh, gave his Lady Dame Margaret Douglas, after him Countess of Bothwell, above two and twenty thousand merks a year of jointure: This, with the pensioner's revenues off the estate, was near thirty six thousand merks a year, which his son Lord Walter, and his son Earl Walter did truely pay all their times the conjunct fee.

Now.

Now, lest you should think that I flatter, or am a liar; I will nominate the lands, and where they lie, for the justification of my self.

Awake, awake, my muse, and me aver,
  ' To give a just account of that jointure,
To the Piel and Hathern I will repair,
To Analshope and Glengeber,
To Whitup and to Black-grain,
To Commonside, and Milsanton-hill,
And Eilridge is left all alone,
Except some town-lands in Lanton.
' Now, my muse, to the east country go we,
And talk of Eckfoord's barony,
Which barony she none did miss,
But all into her jointure was,
In cumulo I do declare,
It's above twenty thousand merks a year;
It was a worthy conjunct fee,
For a Knight to give to his Lady;
That worthy house when they were but gentry,
Exceeded far some of nobility;
O cursed Helena that the Torjans did confound,
And laid Troy's pleasant walls flat on the ground,
Her daughter had not match'd with Priamns' race,
But her mother's persuasion made her him embrace;
Thirty Lairds and Lords it's said hath been,
All of Buckcleugh, yet it is uncertain;
Yet I believe it may be true,
I've seen four my self, and that I'le avow;
The nine last generations I declare,
Both whom they married, and who they were.
At Sir Arthur Scot we begin,
In's time he was the King's warden,

A valiant sp'rit for chivalry,
Married Lord Sommervel's daughter of Cowdalie;
Sir Walter his son did him succeed,
Whom the borders both did fear and dread,
He was still fourty men whenever he rade,
He married with Douglass of Drumlanrig;
Their procreation remains unto this time,
The last honourable second brother, that of that familie came,
From that marriage Robert of Allan-haugh sprung,
It's near two hundred years agone,
And since that time it's known to be of truth,
There was ne're a lawful brother married from Buckcleugh;
The more we may repent, and sigh and groan,
That they'r so Phaenix like still but one.
Sir William Scot was Sir Walter's eldest son,
And in his heritage he did succeed to him,
A valiant knight, and of much renown,
He married with the honourable house of Hume;
His Son Sir Walter, that durst have shown his face,
To him that was as stout as Hercules,
He was inclin'd to blood, as was rehearst,
He was married to Ker of Ferni-harst,
' To Venus her sister, he married again,
' A beautiful creature Dame Janet Beaton;
Sir William Scot of Branksom call'd White-cloak,
He was son to Buckcleugh, call'd Wicked Wat,
As fortune smil'd or frown'd,
Content that Worthy was,
' He married a sister of the house of Angus,
The good Lord Walter was Sir William's son,
The better in Tivot-dale shall never come,
For valour, wisdom, friendship, love, and truth,
' He married Ker a sister of Roxburgh;

Earl

Earl Walter was Lord Walter's son,
A Mars for valour, wisdom and renown,
His courage durst a Lyon fear,
' His frowns would terrifi'd a Boar,
He married a sister of Errol ;
Earl Francis his father, Earl Walter did succeed,
' Into his Earldom, but not to his head ;
Yet he wanted neither hand, head, nor heart,
But could not act like to his father's part ;
His father's acts were all military,
And he was much inclin'd to study ;
His father scorn'd to suffer a stain,
Neither of himself, nor of his name ;
With the house of Rothes married he,
An equal match by antiquitie ;
She was but the relict of such a one,
The son of a start-up soldier new come home.
I have been through Scotland, Holland, and Sweden,
Yet ne're heard of a gentleman in all his kin,
Except one Switzer, which did verifie,
' He was Bacchus nevoy, the uncle of brandy ;
That worthy Earl was soon by death assail'd,
'Gainst whom no mortal ever yet prevail'd.
He had no heirs-male, but daughters left behind,
For to enjoy his great Earldom and land ;
These infants sweet left to their guardians to keep,
Their tutors oft suffered controul,
Their mother was so impudent,
That she must always have her intent ;
The eldest Lady, I confess, she was not able for a man,
With Earl Tarras she did wed, it was by persuasion of her dame ;
Alas, she liv'd not very long ;
' There was no procreation them between ;
I wish to God there had been a son,
It had been better for all poor friends ;

The Countes' sister did her succeed,
Then her mother to London by coach did hie,
And search't her a husband beyond the sea.
A pretty youth, and of high-birth,
By the name of Graves that boy did pass;
One Mr Ross his pedagogue was,
In France, in Holland, and in Flanders,
When the truth was known, and the lad fetcht home,
King Charles the Second's bastard he prov'd to be,
' And I believe his maiden-head, he begat him young on Mrs Barly,
A pretty Lady, I have her seen,
And very gallant in her time;
Sir Thomas Barly was her sire,
A Knight that dwelt in Devonshire,
And after the restauration,
When Charles the Second came to his home,
The Weyms Countess, and her daughter young,
At London stay'd, and the youth fetch'd home,
James Scot he was call'd all along,
Which did continue certain moneths,
And then to Windsor did return,
Where he was made Duke of Monmouth;
King Edward's badge he got, the order of the garter,
Perform'd with great solemnity, and then to London did repair,
His nuptial day did then draw near.
To Charing cross he did resort,
The King and Duke royal did come there;
And most nobles of the court;
A most proper man he in time became,
As in any prince's court was seen,
Ten thousand hearts they may lament,
That ever he should a rebel been;
A rebel he was in his time,
And did the nation much perplex;

At

At his invasion he was tane,
And his head cut off with an ax:
In England now the Dutches dwells,
Which to her friends is a cursed fate,
For if they famish, starve, or die,
They cannot have a groat from that estate.
The times of old are quite forgot,
How inferior friends had still relief,
And how the worthiest of the name
Engaged themselves to hold up their chief,
And in requital of their love,
His honour took of them such pain,
They never went unto the law
'Gainst one another at any time;
In whose case or cause soever it was,
Debts, riots, or possessions,
Their chief he was immediat judge,
The lawyers got nought of them.
Times have been very troublesome,
Since these rebellions first began,
Which was then but fourty eight years agone,
And then our chief he was but young,
In the five and twenty year of 's age,
In the year of grace fifty and two,
He rendered up his Steward-ship,
And had no issue but females two;
And as Dalila with Sampson dealt,
When she cry'd, the Philistines are thee upon,
Such cruel despight, strife, and debat,
Remain into some bad women;
She's like a Gardo countenanc'd like Bendo,
Cunning as Nilo peeping through a window,
Which put the wandring Jew in such amazement,
Seeing such a face look through the casement:

When Lora a Bull long nourished in Cocitus,
With sulphur horns sent by the Emperor Titus,
Asked a stegmatick peribestan question,
If Alexander ever lived physician;
When Helen was for Priamus' son a mate,
From Greece by Paru and his band,
Which caus'd the Greeks the Trojan minds abate:
Some curst the boyes, and other some them ban'd:
The strumpet Queen, which brought the burning brand,
That Helen fir'd, and wrak'd old Priamus race;
And on their names long living shame did brand
For head-strong lusts runs an unbounded race;
This beauteous piece whose feature radiant blaze
Made Mænelaus horn mad war to wadge,
And set all Troy in a combustious bleeze,
Whose ten years triumphs scarce was worth their wage,
For all their conquests, and their battering rams,
' Their leaders most return'd with heads like rams;
Lo thus the burden of adulterous guilt,
A shoring vengeance Troy, and Trojans saw,
No age, nor sect, no beauty, gold nor guilt,
Withstood foretold Cassandria's secret fall;
She often said, false Helen's beauteous blast
Should be the cause, this mighty Grecian's power,
Their names and fames with infamy should blast,
And how the gods on them would vengeance pour;
But poor Cassandra prophesied in vain,
The clamorous crys were to the senseless rocks,
The youths of Troy in mirry scornful vein,
Securely sleeps, while lust the cradle rocks,
Till bloody burning indignation come,
And all their mirth with mourning overcome;
Yet great 's the glory in the noble mind,
Where life and death are equal in respect,
If fates be good or bad, unkind or kind,
Not proud in freedom, nor in thral deject,

With

With courage scorning fortune's worst effect,
In spitting in foul Envy's cankered face,
True honour thus doth baser thoughts subject,
Esteeming life a slave, that serves disgrace;
Foul abject thoughts become the mind that's base,
That deems there is no better life than this,
Or after death doth fear a worser place,
Where guilt is payed the guardian of a miss;
But let swoln Envy swell untill she burst,
The noble mind defys her, do her worst;
The vulgar sort with open port
Said, the Scot had much renown,
That their heretrix was intermixt,
With a bastard of the crown.
King James the Fifth his bastard son
Was of as much regard,
He married Buckcleugh's relict,
He being but a laird.
The bastard got into Scotland,
Was never of such renown,
To prosper as the English do,
They oft usurp their crown;
Kng Arthur of the round table,
Begotten was in adultery;
And so was both King Edelstoun,
And William of Normandie.
But Scotland's loyal nobility
Is of a more rare degree,
Nor suffer any bastard seed
To claim soveraignity.
Since the First Fergus began,
To King James the Seventh,
We have had none but twain,
Of bastards that usurp'd the crown,
And short while they did reign:

Gillis the Tyrant he was one,
King Evenus the first bastard son,
Codallus of Galloway cut him off
In the second year of 's reign;
Duncan the second usurp'd the crown,
Malcolm the third his bastard son,
But from an Usurper he did it gain,
Which was from wicked Donald the Seventh.
Mackpender, then of Merns the Thane,
An Earl of high renown,
He brought King Duncan to his end,
Nine months after he was crown'd.
The bastard Kings of Scotland then
Had but small prosperity,
And for the future I hope none,
In Scotland shall ever be;
Then Edgar the just and lawful king,
Upon his throne was set,
And anointed of Dunkel's Bishop,
Whose name was Mr John Scot.
Of bastards I will speak no more,
Since I declar'd the truth;
My purpose now is to return,
And speak of bold Buckcleugh.
That worthy valiant son of Mars,
That most illustrious one,
The United Provinces him should blaze,
To ages that's to come:
The year and time I must exprime,
That from Holland came he,
The sixteen hundred and thirty three,
At London he did die;
In November month to speak the truth,
It was our woeful fate,

To the Bier many friends came,
To see him ly in state;
The nobles of the court repair'd,
Clad in their sable weed,
And countrymen in flocks came in,
To see's herse when he was dead;
Patrick Scot then of Thirlstone,
A worthy gentleman,
He took the care of all affairs,
Caus'd his corps to be embalm'd,
All being done, that wit of man
Could do or understand;
Then a ship he fraughted on the Thames.
To bring him to Scotland.
The Ship did fall the river down,
And Greenwich did obey;
Then to Gravesend they did come,
And two days there did stay;
When wind and tide they both apply'd,
And hois'd their sails on hie,
Thirlston came abroad himself,
Ere they reach'd Tilburie;
From once they past by the Lands-end,
The storm did rise so high,
For three months time they liv'd in pain,
Sore toil'd upon the sea;
They were almost sunk, yet sav'd the ship at last,
Their sails into the shallow seas were cast,
Yet anchor'd safely and did remain,
Whilst they did put to sea again:
Then 'mongst their old acquaintance storm and flaws,
Each moment near to Death's devouring jaws,
The weary day they past through many fears,
Landed at last quite sunk o're head and ears,

All famish'd, starv'd, like silly rats all drown'd;
From succour far they left their ship on ground,
Cast out their water, whilst they poorly drapt,
' And up and down to dry themselves they hapt.
Thus they their weary pilgrimage did wear,
Expecting for the weather calm and clear:
Then madly, yet study out to the sea they thrust,
'Gainst wind and storms so hie,
By Prignal hidden rocks which hidden ly,
Ten mile within the sea, some wet, some dry,
There they supposed their danger most of all,
If they upon these ragged rocks should fall:
But Sol, that old continual traveller,
From Titan can amount his flaming car,
The weather kept his course with fire, hail, and rage,
Without appearance that it would e're aswage;
Whilst they did pass these hills, dails, and downs,
Every moment they looked to be drown'd,
The wind still blowing and the sea so hie,
As if the lofty waves would kiss the skie,
That many times they wish'd with all their hearts,
Their ship were sunk, and they in landwart carts,
Or any part to kep them safe and dry,
The water raged so outragiously;
For it is said since memory of man,
Or since winds and seas to ebb and flow began,
No man can mind of such stormy weather,
And continual rage so long together;
Thirteen long weeks that many thought,
The wind blew south and south-west,
And rais'd the sea each wave above another,
Of fair and calm weather not an hour together,
And whither they did go by Sun or Moon,
Either by midnight or by noon:

The

The sun did rise with most suspicious face,
Of foul forbidding weather purple red,
His radiant tincture east-north-east were spread;
In Norway by Slewgates antient castle,
Against rugged rocks and waves they tug'd,
The moon and stars were covered under cloud;
By Rubnie and by Rubnie-marsh,
The tide against them, and the wind was harsh;
'Twixt Eolus and Neptune there was such strife,
That men never such weather in their life,
' Tost and retost, retost and tost again,
With rumbling and tumbling on the rowling main;
The boisterous breaking billows of the curl'd locks,
Did impetuously beat against the rocks;
The wind, which like a horse, whose wind is broke,
Blew thick and short, that they were almost choack'd,
As it outrageously the billows waves,
The gust like dust blown in the brimish waves;
And thus the wind and seas these boysterous gods,
Fell by the ears stark mad at furious odds;
There Stalward ships turmoil'd 'twixt shoars and seas,
Aloft, or low, as storms and floodsdid please;
Sometimes upon a foaming mountain top,
Whose hight did seem the heav'n to under-prop;
Then straight to such prophanity they fell,
As if they div'd into the depths of hell;
The clouds like ryp apostoms burst and shower'd,
Their matt'ry, watry substance head-long pour'd:
Yet though all things were mutable and fickle,
' They all agreed to sauce them in a pickle;
Of water fresh and salt from seas and skies,
Which with our sweat joyned in triplicty,
Bright Phoebus hid his golden head with fear,
Not daring to behold the dangers there;

Whilst in that strait and exigent they stand,
They see and wish to land, yet durst not land,
Like rowling hills the billows beat and roar,
Against the melancholy benchy shoar;
That if they landed, neither strength nor wit,
Could save their ship from being sunk or split;
To keep the sea straight puffing Æolus breath,
Did threaten still to blow them unto death,
The waves amain oft boarded them,
Whilst they almost six hours did there remain;
On every side with danger and distress,
Resolv'd to run a shore a dungeonness;
There stood some thirteen cottages together,
To shelter poor fisher-men from wind and weather;
And there some people were, as they supposed,
As though the doors and windows were all closed;
They near the land, into the sea soon lap,
To see what people there these houses kept;
They knockt and call'd at each from house to house,
But found no mankind-form, cat, rat, nor mouse;
These news all sad, and comfortless and cold,
Amongst the crew it presently was told,
Assuring them, the best way they did think,
Was to leave the ship, whether she split or sink:
Resolved thus, they altogether please
To put her head to shore, and her stern to seas;
They leaping over-board amidst the sea,
Almost desperate whether to live or dy;
Then from top to toe they streud,
Pluckt off their shirts, and then them wring'd,
Till sun and wind their want supply'd,
And made both outside and inside dry'd:
Two miles from thence, a silly town their stood,
To which they went to bring some food:

The

The town did shew their pity, but for what?
They made them pay triple for what they got;
But what they got Thirlston stood not for to pay double;
But these peasants made him to pay twice triple,
Because these harbours where their ship rode still,
Belong'd to men which in that town did dwell:
At Thirlston's request they did send a man,
To possess the crew in that hospitable den,
With a brazen kettle, and a wooden dish,
To serve their need, and dress their flesh and fish:
Then from the fleshers they brought lamb and sheep,
Ale from the Ostler-house, and besoms for to sweep;
Their cottage for want of usage was moisty,
Myrish, sluggith, and dusty;
' There twenty days they did roast, boil, and broil,
' And toil, and moyle, and keep a noble coyle:
For only they keept open house alone,
And he that wanted beef, might eat a stone:
Their Grand-dame Earth with beds did all befriend them;
And bountifully all their lengths did lend them;
That laughing or else lying down did make,
Their back and sides sore, and their ribs to ake.
Meantime in the town Thirlston did remain,
His lodging was little better than them.
On Saturnday the winds did seem to cease,
And brawling seas began to hold their peace:
Then they like tenants beggarly and poor,
Intended to leave the key beneath the door:
But that the landlord did that shift prevent,
Who came in pudding time and took his rent.
Then Thirlston came before the sun was peeping,
They lanch'd to sea, and left their house keeping,
When presently they saw the drifting skys,
Grin pout and lowr and winds and seas 'gain rise,

Country-men wish Thirlston go by land,
To a harbour that was near at hand;
The name of it was Fresenbered,
And there their ship might by report be reared:
But their council was not worth a plack,
He'd never leave the ship, to ride on horse's back:
Yet fortune brought them to the harbour there,
Where that their ship they somewhat did repair,
And then to sea, with mounted sails on hie,
The bound for Scotland, and left Norway:
There was but small amendment all that time,
The weather was much in one kind.
The wind and weather plaid on each so wild,
As if they meant not to be reconcil'd;
She, whilst they leapt upon these liquid hills,
Where purpoises did shew their phins and gills:
Yet after that, both water, wind, and seas,
And a pleasant gale blew from the north north-east.
Æolus and Neptune privat, and no way brief;
' By providence they did arrive at Leith.
That troublesome, toilsome journey, to be brief,
' Fifteen weeks was between London and Leith.
To all ages it should ne're be forgot,
The pains that Patrick Scot of Thirlston took.
Æneas on Anchises he took pains enough,
' But Patrick Scot he took more of the Earl of Buckcleugh:
All that men can do, when princes do command,
Their loyalty to show, and venture life and land:
I have known many on Buckcleugh's means was bred,
Yet one night, from home, they never lay from bed.

THE END OF THE FIRST PART.

SATCHELS'S POSTRAL,

HUMBLY PRESENTED

TO HIS

Noble and Worthy Friends of the Names of SCOT and ELLIOT, and others.

PART SECOND.

EDINBURGH: Printed by the Heir of ANDREW ANDERSON, Printer to His Most Sacred Majesty, City and Colledge, 1688; and reprinted by BALFOUR & SMELLIE, 1776.

To the truly Worthy, Honourable, and Right Worshipful Sir Francis Scot of Thirlston, Knight-Baronet, wishes Earth's honour and Heaven's happiness.

> THIS book, good Sir, the issue of my brain,
> Though far unworthy of your worthy view,
> In hope ye gently it will intertain,
> Yet I in duty offer it to you;
> Although the method and the phrase be plain,
> Not art, like writ, as to the stile is due,
> And truth I know your favour will obtain;
> The many favours I have had from you,
> Hath forc'd me thus to show my thankful mind,
> And of all faults I know no vice so bad,
> And hateful as ungratefully inclin'd;
> A thankful heart is all a poor man's wealth,
> Which with this book I give your worthy self:
> I humbly crave your worthiness excuse,
> This boldness of my poor unlearned muse,
> That hath presum'd so high a pitch to fly,
> In praise of virtue and gentility:
> I know this task's most fit for learned men,
> For Homer, Ovid, or for Virgil's pen;
> These lines I have presum'd to dite,
> It's known to your Honour I could never write.

> > Your Honour's most obedient servant,

> > > WALTER SCOT of Satchels.

SATCHELS'S POST'RAL:

Humbly presented to his Noble and Worthy Friends of the Names of Scot *and* Elliot.

⁂⁂⁂⁂⁂⁂⁂⁂⁂⁂⁂⁂⁂⁂⁂

WHEN restless Phœbus seem'd himself to rest,
His flaming car descending to the west,
And high Spyro obscured his twinckling light;
Then in a sable mantle Madam Night,
Took of the world the sole command and keep,
Charging the eyes of mortals fast asleep :
She send dull Morphæus forth ; and summons both,
The Leaden Potentates of sleep and slouth,
Who unto every one good rest imparts,
Save lovers guilty minds, and careful hearts ;
The stealing hours crep't on with sleeping pace,
When masked Mid-night shewed her ebon'd face,
When hags and furies, witches, faries, elfs,
Ghosts, sp'rits and goblins do separat themselves ;
When fond imaginary dreams do reign,
In formless forms, in men's molested brain ;
An un-accustomed dream came in my head,
I thought as it were near by a river side,
Within a pleasant grove I did abide,
That all the feathered birds that sweems and flees,
Betwixt the breeding earth and skyes,
One at the least of every several sort,
Did for their recreation there resort ;

S   Then

Then there was such varieties of notes,
Such whirling and such whistling from their throats,
The baess, the tenor, treble and the main,
All acting various actions in one strain.
I thought twenty four sheperds did draw near,
To hear the musick of that feath'red quire;
These feather'd fidlers change their notes most sweet,
And lull'd Apollo's daughters fast asleep;
Mean time the shepherds tript upon the mould,
Their flocks they did remain in Cupid's fold,
And the four and twenty did appear,
In three squadrons, like martial men of wear:
If that my memory fail me not,
They were friends and kindred of the name of Scot:
' It's my happy hap to be
' Of these Scots relations,
' Therefore I'le dyte their pedegree
' To the eight or ninth generations.

TO speak the truth, no man shall me controul,
    Of worthy Garrenberry, Rennal-burn and wall,
Todrick, and Gilmans-cleugh they were in my dream,
And good Grass-yards, and Adam in Delorian,
William in Milsinstoun, a gentleman of note,
And worthy Gaudy-lands, and Wauchops Walter Scot;
Sheills-wood and Langup also did appear,
And Henry Scot of Palace-hill he call'd up the rear:
These appeared to be Scots, who in the first squad came;
' The second squad was Elliots, I was not so well acquaint with them.
    The second squad that appeared all into my Dream,
Was the name of Elliot, and all fine Gentlemen;
I am not vers'd to know from whence they came,
But sure at first they seem'd most from Las'distoun;
Except John Elliot, where I have had good cheer,

That

That dwells in Unthank, he's brother to Dunlibyre;
The rest of their pedegree, I know them not,
Except Bewly and Muckldean that's related to Scot.
  The third squad are men that's void of harms,
For they are shepherds swains trained up from bairns;
It is their daily exercise and gain,
To tend all sort of sheep, weather, ew, and ram;
That name of shepherd swain came first from Greece,
As plainly doth appear, by Jason's golden fleece;
Although it be not well, I caused insert't with speed,
The faillings of a fool, it is no cause of feed,
Sage wisdom should accept the will for the deed;
Had I Ovid's muse, and Virgil's vein,
And wit to use Ulysses pen,
T'extoll these shepherds swains, I would incline,
From Titan's rise, according to my dream.
To John Elliot in Unthank in a storm, I came late,
But now to Henry of Hare-wood I mind for to skip,
And to his brother John, and John of Thorslee-hope,
To see William Elliot of Swinside, it is my full desire,
And good John Elliot in Unthank that's brother to Dunlibyre;
Walter Elliot of Erkelton, he is a man of note;
'So is Muckildean his brother, he's son to Janet Scot,
Robert Elliot in Diuslees, the Laird of Clacks his Frier,
And good William Elliot of Bewly, he drives up the rear;
'The rear's the second place, if souldiers be but stout,
'He is sure to have the van, if the word be face about;
This was the second squad appeared into my dream.
  This is the third consciencious squad,
My author doth me assure,
Although they be but shepherd swains,
They do relieve the poor;
As for John Grieve in Garwold,
He keeps both board and bed,

So doth James Grieve in Lennup,
And the Grieves on Common side :
And it is true, John Robertson,
Is a comerad good enough,
And for house keeping he excels,
He dwells in Cauterscleugh ;
Wheat-bread, salt-beef, mutton, and old cheese,
I riding by, he did my hungar ease,
With capon, and lamb, brandy and good ale,
He feasted me in May, as I had been an Earl :
George Curror in Hartwood-myres,
He is a religious man ;
So is Michael Andison in Annalshope,
And his brother John in Thirlston ;
John Tod that dwells in Tushilaw
Can many sheep afford ;
And Thomas Anderson is not small,
That dwells in the How-foord.
Unto my dream, these were the men,
Which did appear to me,
They were four and twenty at the first,
But since I've added three.

Dedicated to the Right Honourable Walter *Earl of* Tarras.

My Lord,

THE lives and deaths of Knights, Lords and Earls,
This little book unto your Honour tells,
Protection and acceptance if you give,
It shall, as shall yourself, for ever live ;
Of all the wonders this vile world includes,
I muse how flatt'ry such high favour gains,
How adulation cunningly deludes
Both high and low from scepter to the swain,

But

Post'ral.

But if thou by flatt'ry couldst obtain,
More than the most that is possest by men,
Thou could'st not tune thy tongue to falsehood strain,
Yet with the best can use both tongue and pen,
Thy secret learning can both scan and ken,
The hidden things of nature and of art,
It's thou hast rais'd me from oblivion's den,
And made my muse from obscure sleep to start;
And to your Honour's censure I commit,
The first-born issue of my worthless wit,
Fresh-water souldiers sails in shallow streams,
' And Leith-wynd captains venture not their lives,
A brain disturb'd brings furth idle dreams,
And guilded sheaths have seldom golden knives,
And painted faces none but fools bewitch,
My muse is plain but witty, fair, and rich:
When thou didst first to Aganipa float,
Without thy knowledge as I surely think,
Where grace and nature filling up thy fountain,
My muse came flowing from Parnassus' mountain;
So long may she flow as it to thee is fit,
The boundless ocean of a Christian wit:
For wit, reason, grace, religion, nature, zeal,
Wrought altogether in thy working brain,
And to thy work did set this certain seal,
Pure is the colour that will take no stain:
My Lord, although I do transgress,
You know that I did never yet profess,
Untill this time in print to be a poet,
And now to exercise my wit I show it;
View but the intrals of this little book,
And you will say that I some pains have took,

T   Pains

Pains mix'd with pleasure, pleasure join'd with pain,
Produc'd this issue of my lab'ring brain.
My dear Lord, to you I owe a countless debt,
Which though I ever pay, will ne're be payed.
'Tis not base coin, subject to canker's fret,
If so in time my debt might be defray'd;
But this my debt I would have all men know,
Is love, the more I pay the more I owe;
Wit, learning, honesty, and all good parts,
Hath so possess'd thy body and thy mind,
That covetously thou steals away mens hearts,
Yet 'gainst thy shaft there's never one repay'd:
My heart that is my greatest worldly pelf,
Shall ever be for thee as for myself;
Thou that in idle adulating words,
Canst never please the humours of these days,
That greatest works with smallest speech afford,
Whose wit the rules of wisdom's love obeys;
In few words then, I wish that thou mayst be,
As well belov'd of all men as of me.
To vertue and to honour once in Rome,
Two stately temples there erected was,
Where none might into honour's temple come,
But first through vertue's temple they must pass;
Which was an emblem and an document,
That men by vertue must true honour win;
And how that honour shall be permanent,
Which only did from vertue first begin.
Could envy die if honour were deceas'd,
She could not live for honour's envy's food,
She lives by sucking of the noble blood,
And scales the lofty top of fame's high crest,
Base thoughts compacted in the object's breast,

The meager monster doth neither harm nor good,
But like the wain, or wax, or ebb, or flood,
She shuns as what her age doth most detaste,
Where heaven-bred honour in the noble mind,
From out the cavern of the breast proceeds,
Ther hell-born envy shews her hellish kind,
And vulture-like upon the actions feed ;
But here's the odds, that honour's tree shall grow
When envy's rotten stump shall burn in low.
   My Lord, I know your Honour knows,
That I must speak the truth ;
John Scot he was a natural son,
To Walter Earl of Buckcleugh,
Begot on Madam Drummond,
A noble lady by birth,
By kindred cousin-german
To the right honourable Earl of Perth :
He promis'd her wedlock, and prov'd unto her so,
' As Prince Æneas did to the Carthage Queen Dido ;
But yet let their succession
Live still in memory,
He was a worthy valiant squire,
' John Scot of Gorinberry ;
At the beauty of all the nine,
He hit the mark,
And married Sir John Liddle's daughter,
' Knight Baron, and Baronet ;
And betwixt these worthy couple, procreat there be,
This present Francis Scot, the good laird of Gorinberry
He hath gain'd the constant and true Penelope,
He's married to Sir John Wachop's daughter,
That old baron of Niddrie,
Whose names and fames, birth and antiquity,
Surpasses many ladies of some nobility ;

I have declar'd the family,
Of the worthy lairds of Gorinberry,
And hopes his honour thinks no shame,
For to be call'd a shepherd's swain.

Our father Adam's second son, a prince
As great as any man begotten since,
Yet in his function he a shepherd was,
And so his mortal pilgrimage did pass :
And in the secret text it is compil'd,
That he that's father of the faithful stil'd,
Did as a shepherd live upon th' increase
Of sheep on earth, until his days did cease ;
And in these days it was apparent then,
' Abel and Abram both were noblemen :
The one obtained his title righteously,
For his unfeigned serving the Most High ;
He first did offer sheep, which on record
Was sacrifice accepted of the Lord,
Since patriarchs were shepherds
In Arcadia, and Greece,
I wish the wool in Etherston-sheils,
May grow like Jason's fleece.

Dedicated to the very Honourable, and Right Worshipful Sir Francis
Scot *of* Thirlston.

SIR, my weak collections out hath took,
' The sum and pith of sundry chronicle books ;
For pardon and protection I intreat,
The volume's little, but my presumption's great.
Sir, since all memorandums of fore past ages,
Sayings, and sentences of antient sages,
The glory of Apollo's radiant chine
The supporter of the sacred sisters nine,

The

The Attullus that all historians do bear,
Throughout the world, here and every where;
Whoever went behind you, I would ken,
Whose worth throughout the spacious nation ring.
Since Rennal-burn, your worship's kinsman near,
He hath those sheep which golden fleeces wear,
And it may be, it is such beast and fleece,
Which Jason brought from Cholcos into Greece;
John Scot the squire of Newburgh-hall,
Alias of Rennal-burn as men him call,
To the first John Scot of Rennal-burn late,
He was the son and heir to his estate,
Who was the son of that Sir John Scot of worth,
The prince of poets, and knight of Newburgh,
Chancer Glovet, and Sir Thomas Moir,
And Sir Philip Sidney, who the lawrel wear,
They never had a more poetical vein,
Than Newburgh's John, that was Mr Arthur's son.
And Mr Arthur was a learned man,
Son to Simon Scot of Newburgh then.
This Simon Scot's call'd Simon with the spear,
Tutor of Thirlston was both for peace and wear;
That Simon Scot, a bold and resolute man,
He was son to John Scot of Thirlston;
John Scot of Thirlston,
My guid-sir let me knaw,
He was son to David Scot of Howpaslaw;
That David Scot he did excell,
'Mongst all hunters he bore the bell;
He did abound for wit and skill;
All his associates did wear a tod tail;
Which they esteem most by their engadges,
More than French Gallants do of their plumages.
David of Howpaslaw, he was the son
Of the first Sir Walter, e're was of that roum,

He was a man of credit and renown,
' He married Elliot daughter to the Laird of Lariston ;
David of Howpaslaw, Sir Walter's son,
He married with Scot, a daughter of Robertoun ;
His son John Scot of Thirlston a man of worth,
He married Scot, the daughter of the Laird of Allenhaugh.
John's son, Robert, was warden in his time,
The fight of Robert's hill he did gain ;
He for his king, and country, did maintain the truth ;
He married Scot, daughter to the Laird of Buckcleugh ;
The first Sir Robert Scot of Thirlston was his son,
He married Margaret, daughter to the Laird of Cranston ;
Sir Robert Scot his son, for whose death I mourn,
He married Lyon, daughter to the master of Kinghorn.
His death was sad to all his near relations,
A worthy man was he,
And died without succession :
Then Patrick Scot, his father-brother son.
Took on the designation of Thirlston.
A very worthy courteous man was he,
He married Murray daughter to the Laird of Blackbarony ;
His son Sir Francis Scot, Knight Baronet of Thirlston,
Is now married to Ker, daughter to William Earl of Louthian.
Of his genealogy I said enough,
His original it is of Buckcleugh ;
Yet were it no more but so I dare be bold,
To think this land doth many Jasons hold ;
Who never yet did pass a dangerous wave,
Yet may with ease its golden fleeces have.
' My little book whoso doth entertain,
' It's dedicat to none but gentlemen ;
' Sometimes to old, sometimes to young,
' Sometimes to the father, sometimes to the son,
' Sometimes to the great, sometimes to the small,
' So my book it keeps no rule at all.

Dedicated

Dedicated to that worthy and compleat gentleman, Robert Scot, *second son to* Sir William Scot *of* Hardin.

UNLEARNED Azo store of books hath bought,
  Because a learned scholar he'l be thought;
I counsell'd him that had of books such store,
To buy pipes, flutes, the viol, and bandore,
And then his music, and his learning share,
Being both alike, with either might compare;
He did both beat his brain, and try his wit,
In hopes thereby to please the multitude;
As soon may ride a horse without a bit,
Above the moon or sun's high altitude;
Then neither flattery, nor the hope of pelf,
Hath made me writ, but for to please myself:
Though sin and hell work mortals to betray,
Yet 'gainst thy malice, God still arms thy way;
Thou canst behave amongst those banks and briers,
As well as he who to cedars-top aspires,
Or to the lowest cherub, or branch of broom,
That hath its breeding from earth's stumbling womb.
And now I talk of broom, of shrubs and cedars,
Me thinks a world of trees, are now my leaders.
To prosecute this travel made with pain,
And make comparison betwixt trees and men;
The cedars, and the high-clouds kissing pines,
Fœcunds, olives, and the crooked vines,
The elm, the esk, the oak, the mastie beech,
The pear, the apple, and the rough gound peach;
And many more, for it would tedious be,
To name each fruitful and unfruitful tree.
For to proceed, and shew how men and trees,
In birth and breed, in life and death agrees.

In their beginning they have both one birth,
Both have their natural being from the earth;
Those that scape fortune, and the extreams of love,
Unto their longest home by death are drove,
Where Cesars, Kesars, subjects objects most,
Be all alike consum'd to dirt and dust:
Death endeth all our cares, or cares increase,
It sends us unto lasting pain, or bless;
Where honour is with noble vertue mixt;
It like a rock stands permanent and fix't.
The snares of Envy, or her traps of hate,
Could never, nor shall ever hurt that state.
Like adamant it beats back the battery,
Of spightful malice, and deceiving flattery.
For it with pride can never be infected,
But humbly is supernally protected;
A supporter, or prop I wish Robert be,
As Rowlin call'd Robert was to Normandy.
Robert call'd John-Fernyear was in Scotland,
So was Robert Bruce his revenging powerful hand.
I wish thee health, wealth, and renown,
Without any expectation of a crown:
This dedication which to your hands takes scop,
Concerns a shepherd from Will Scot of Langup,
Who's a prudent, wise, and civil gentleman,
As many that lives in this part of the land;
Who sprung from a worthy stock of late,
Who was named John Scot of Langup,
Who was the son, I very well knew,
Of John Scot of Headshaw;
And John Scot, we all do ken,
Was son to George Scot of Sinton;
And George Scot, called How-coat,
Was son of Sinton's youngest Wat;

And

And Young Wat was Walter's son,
That was Laird of Sinton, whence Hardin sprung,
And Walter he was George son,
And George he was the son of John;
For Walter and William was too brether,
His name was George that was their father.
My memory is Lord-keeper of my treasure,
And great understanding gives true justice measure,
To good, to bad, to just and to unjust,
Invention and remembrance waits the leasure
Of memory and understanding most,
Hath wisdom for her fellow and her guide;
Else princes, peers, and commons stray aside:
For William Scot in our south part of Greeces,
I wish may ne're want such as Jason's golden fleeces.

Dedicated to the worthy and well accomplished gentleman, William Scot *of* Rae-burn.

THE justice, mercy, and the might I sing,
Of heaven's just, merciful, almighty king,
By whose fore-knowledge all things were elected,
Whose power hath all things made, and all projected;
Whose mercies flood hath quencht his justice flame,
Who is, shall be, one, and still the same.
Who in the prime, when all things first began,
Made all for man, and for himself made man:
Made, not begotten, or of human birth,
No seir but God, no mother but the earth,
Who ne're knew childhood, or the sucking-teat,
But at the first was made a man compleat;
Whose inward soul in God-like form did shine,
As image of the majesty divine;
Whose super-natural wisdom beyond nature,
' Did name each sensible and senseless creature;

And from whose star-like, sand-like generation,
Sprung every kindred, kingdom, tribe and nation.
All people then one language spoke alone,
Interpreters the world then needed none;
There lived then no learned deep grammarians,
There was no Turks, no Scythians, nor Tartarians;
Then all was one, and one was only one,
The language of the universal ball;
Then if a traveller had gone as far,
As from the Artick to the Antartick star,
If he from Boreas into Auster went,
Or from the Orient to the Occident,
Which way so ever he did turn or wind,
He had been sure his country-man to find;
One hundred thirty winters since the flood,
The earth one only language understood,
Until the son of Cush, the son of Cham,
A proud cloud-scaling tower began to frame,
Trusting, that if the world again were drown'd,
He in his lofty building might rest sound;
All future floods he purpos'd to prevent,
Aspiring to heaven's glorious battlement;
' But high Jehovah with a puft was able,
' To make ambitious Bable but a bable.
These shepherd swains, I send into your view,
Are thirty one, a very worthy crew;
Fifteen of them are gentlemen of note,
All of the renown'd name of Scot;
Whereof Henry Scot in Palishil is one,
The youngest shepherd swain of all the name
He's natural son unto that bold Barron.
Sir John Scot the knight of Ancrum;

Both

Both wealth and wisdom his father doth embrace,
And he abounds in Jason's golden fleece.

Dedicated to the illustrious and worthy gentleman, Thomas Scot *of* Whitslade.

MOST worthy Sir, I have with pain and labour took,
To search some histories for this little book,
I have it all gathered from thence,
' Especially things of greatest consequence;
And though the volume, and the work be small,
Yet it does contain the sum of all;
To you I give it, with a heart most fervent,
And rests your humble and obedient servant.
    For shepherd swains they have been long
The glory of their land,
The best of men has been a swain,
Behold brave Tamerlane;
Then Walter Scot now of Todrick,
Since thou'rt a gentleman,
I'm sure thou'll not offended be,
To be call'd a shepherd's swain;
Thy father Thomas did the like,
Since he to Todrick came:
Thomas thy good-sir was a swain,
When he from Whitslade sprung:
Thy grandsire brave Walter of Whitslade
Was call'd the hawk compleat,
A man of note and good report,
Yet had many flocks of sheep;
His father Robert thy great grandsir,
Of Stirches was design'd,
Because his father Walter Scot
Liv'd at Whitslade, in his time

He was a worthy gentleman,
And kept a great Menzie:
There was ninety years past o're his head
Before that he did die;
The rest of thy genealogie,
I can you well declare,
They were all worthy gentlemen :
But I will talk no mair.

 To speak of Whitslade's family
Or when it did begin,
It's above two hundred years ago;
It was in the fourteen hundred eighty seven,
Walter the first of Whitslade then,
Was Hardin's elder brother,
He married a fair comely dame,
Daughter to the Laird of Riddel;
Robert his father did succeed,
In heretages, mains, and miln,
And married with one Rutherford,
Daughter to the Laird Hunthill;
His son Walter, sharp as a hawk.
For valour he did pass,
He married with a comely dame,
Daughter to Caver's of Dowglas;
His son Sir Walter Scot, if I should forget,
I should be much to blame,
He married with Susanna Scot,
Daughter to the Laird of Thirlston;
And after her he married again,
Which I do know for truth,
Unto a very comely lass,
Sister to Sir John Scot of Newburgh:

His

His son Robert Scot of worthy note,
' Holland's Jean married he,
Natural daughter to Walter Lord of Buckcleugh,
She was a frugal lady.
Sir Walter Scot, brother to Robert,
He married a Lady fair,
Daughter to Sir Robert Stuart of Ormstoun,
' Which is brother to John Earl of Traquair;
Thomas his brother did him succeed,
A man of worthy fame,
A verteous Lady he did wed,
Madam Mitchel was her name.
Thomas his son doth now remain,
The eighth Laird of that part,
He's married to a frugal dame,
Daughter to Sir John Hay of Park.
Thomas the last that of Whitslade we lost,
Was a man of good esteem,
He departed in the year of grace
Sixteen hundred and seventy one.
Sir Walter Scot his brother, that
At Innerkeithing was slain,
It was into the year of grace
Sixteen hundred and fifty one;
His brother Robert that bold barron,
It was an woful hour,
At York's great fight he lost his life,
In the sixteen hundred and forty four.
Their father brave Sir Walter Scot,
The chief of chivalry,
In the sixteen hundred twenty eighth year,
At Whitslade he did die.
Of Whitslade's worthy family,
I will no further dite,
For he does know assuredly,
I can neither read nor write.

Ulysses was a happy man of men,
In that his acts were writ with Homer's pen;
And Virgil wrote the actions of the glory,
Of brave Æneas and his wandring story;
The shepherds live, and thus they end their lives,
With good and brave and just prerogatives.

Dedicated to that worthy gentleman, John Scot *of* Wall, *brother german to* Sir William Scot *of* Hardin *elder.*

MOST worthy Sir, into your hands I give,
  The sum of that which makes me so brief,
I humbly crave acceptance at your hand,
And rests your servant ever to command.
  Since I've begun, I hope to make an end,
And as I can my shepherd swains defend;
For Walter Scot of Wall,
These lines I do design;
For there are many gallants
That have shepherds been;
Rome's fond Romulus was bred and fed,
'Mongst shepherds where his youthful days he led.
The Persian Monarch Cyrus he did pass,
His youth with shepherds, and a shepherd was;
Wherefore I humbly thee intreat,
' If I do call thee shepherd, not to fret;
For I know ye are all gentlemen,
To the seventh or eighth generation:
And I will do to you that I'll not do to others,
' For I'll describe you both your fathers and mothers;
Because erroneous liars the old family did not ken,
Call'd Harden, this and that said, they're not gentlemen;
Wherefore I will at William begin,
Brother german to Walter of Sinton.

Who was a man of great command,
He enjoyed all Sinton's Lordship,
And the Beat-up land;
He was the son of George,
Who did enjoy the same,
So did his father, his name was John:
George left his second son, it is most clear,
'Twixt four and five thousand merks a year,
Into that possession at that time,
I know not what charter and evidence was then:
Yet to let misbelieving people ken,
These lands as they ly, I will design;
Therefore William was a valiant man,
Who was the first laird of Hardin:
In his possession he had then no less
Nor Hardin, Totshaw, Mebenlaw, and High-chesters.
With Todrick, which good sheep afford;
Wester-Essenside, Burnfoot, and Sheillswood;
These were the lands I do explain,
That George of Sinton gave his son William;
Why should ramping liars blast his fame,
And say that he was not a gentleman;
He wanted nothing of gentry,
But only the title of dignity:
The first lady that he did gain,
Was daughter to the baron of Chism,
' Then in Hardin place he did sit down,
' And on her there begat one only son;
For within short process of swift time,
She dy'd ere she came to her prime:
The laird a widower did remain,
How long a time I do not ken;
But his son he grew up to be a man,
The first Walter Scott of Hardin:

Then

Then Hardin did to Riddel ride,
The old laird of Riddel being dead,
In suit of his relict there came he,
She was a daughter of Fairnilie;
She was a fair and a beauteous dame,
And at that time she was but young;
Her beauty others did excell,
She had one daughter to Riddel,
Brave William Scot he did her gain,
They had not been long in that roum,
While the ladie's daughter married the laird's son;
Then they left the young folk in Hardin,
And the old folk in Todrick they sat down,
' And there they did two sons beget,
' Robert of Burnfoot, and George of Todrick;
And both of them prov'd stout able men,
They were the first cadents come of Hardin:
Now to the young folks I return,
The Laird and Lady of Hardin,
Betwixt them was procreat a son,
Call'd William Bolt-foot of Hardin;
He did survive to be a man,
And then to the Fairnilie he came;
And Fairnilie's daughter he did wed;
For they were related by kindred:
Betwixt them two was procreat,
The stout and valiant Walter Scot
Of Hardin, who can never dy,
But live by fame to the tenth degree:
He became both able, strong and stout,
Married Philip's daughter, squire of Dryhope,
Which was an antient family,
And many broad lands enjoyed he;
Betwixt these Scots was procreat,
That much renown'd Sir William Scot.

I need not to explain his name,
Because he ever lives by fame:
He was a man of port and rank,
He married Sir Gideon Murray's daughter of Elibank;
Betwixt them there was procreat,
This old Sir William that's living yet:
This old Sir William married
A sister of the house of Boyd,
And there's procreat them betwixt,
Sir William Scott, now call'd youngest,
' Because his father does remain,
' Therefore he's called young Sir William;
And young Sir William married
The only daughter of Sir John Nisbet,
He late was advocat to the King,
And now is call'd Lord Dirltoun:
This genealogy is true,
And the old was as good as the new.
Now worthy Wall, I wish thee life and health,
Hoping thou'l ne're marry inferior to thyself;
Yet ambition, pomp, and hell-begotten pride,
And damn'd adulation thou will still deride;
The complimental flattery of kings courts
I hope shall ne're be mixt amidst thy sports:
For Homer was the prime of poets stil'd,
And worthy actions still he did compile;
That he did both in Arcadia and Greece,
Extol the shepherds with Jason's golden fleece.

Dedicated to the Honourable and well accomplished gentleman, Sir William, Scot *of* Hardin Knight.

UNTO the prospect of your wisdom's eyes,
   I consecrat these silly lines,

Not that I think them worthy of your view,
But, because in love my thoughts are bound to you ;
I do confess myself unworthy far,
To dite in such like cases as they are:
Which Homer, Virgil, nor the fluent Tullie,
In fitting terms could scarce express them fully:
For Francis Scot of Gilman's-cleugh,
To you I do commend,
In hoeps your worship still will be his friend,
The son of John, the son of Robert, call'd Truth,
Who was the son of James,
The first of Gilman's-cleugh,
A valiant gentleman, who well deserv'd renown,
He was the youngest son to John Scot of Thirlston ;
The which John Scot he did excell,
Being son to David with the tod's tail ;
And David Scot, my author let me know,
He was son to Walter of Howpaslaw :
Sir Walter he was William's son,
Of the worthy house of Buckcleugh he sprung,
The lads in Gilman's-cleugh,
In hunting did excell ;
So did their father David,
That carried the tod's tail,
Who had as much delight,
In hunting of that beast,
As Jason had in Greece
To bear the Golden fleece.

Dedicated to the Right Hnourable, Sir John Scot *of* Ancrum, *Knight, wishes mirth and happiness be still your attendance.*

T H E guns proclaim'd aloud on every hill,
　　The joyful acclamations of the Scots People ;

　　　　　　　　　　　　　　　　　　　　　　The

The which did thunder with so high a strain,
As if great Mars they meant to entertain:
True mirth and gladness was to every face,
And healths run bravely round in every place;
That sure I think the seventh day of July,
At the Reid-swair should ne're foregotten be;
That was a day to his everlasting fame,
The valiant Laird Wat brought in the worthy name;
That day should ever be dedicat to mirth,
As if it had been a soveraign's birth:
When valiant Wat, that worthy man,
Brought in the name of Scot, well to been seen;
It was nothing ye'll say to bring them in,
But to th' effusion of his blood
He brought them back again;
The executors and tutors, that hath been in our time,
The honour of the Scots did ne're so much proclaim:
The old verse I must give in,
' Though men should say that I am drunken,
How Watt thy guid-sir, that worthy man,
To the Reid-swair brought his troop,
The seventh day of July, the sooth to say,
At the Reid-swair the tryst was set;
Our wardens they did fix a day,
As they appointed, so they met.
The Lord Buckcleugh he was but young,
Carmichael was warden in his place,
The Laird Wat, that worthy man,
Commanded the sirname with great grace:
Thy pedegree is soon described,
I think I may do it well enough.
Thy father Charles was Laird Wat's son,
Who was natural son to Scot of Buckcleugh,
Their generations is formerly described.

I need them not describe again,
Both Walter's and William's and Sir Arthur;
Unto the ninth generation;
From whence such men may gather their relief,
That though a ram-head may be cause of grief,
Yet nature hath a remedy found out,
They should have Lyons hearts to bear it out;
Though I call'd thee shepherds swain,
Yet I deserve no blame;
I hope that Jason's golden-fleece
With thee still shall remain.

Dedicated to the right worshipful, and very honourable, and most generous gentleman, Sir William Scot *of* Hardin *younger.*

THE Prince of Princes, and the King of Kings,
    Whose eye of providence foresees all things,
To whom, whatever was, or ever shall be,
I present still before his Majesty,
Who doth dispose of all things as he list,
' And graspeth time in his eternal fist;
He sees and knows for us what's bad or good,
And all things is by him well understood,
Mens weak conjecture no man can arreid.
What in th' eternal parliaments decreed;
And what the Trinity concludeth there,
We must expect it with obedience here;
Then let not any man presume so far,
To search what the Almightie's councils are;
But let our wills attend upon his will,
And let his will be our direction still:
Let not Plebeians be inquisitive,
Nor into any profound state business dive.

We

We into the thousand and sixteenth year,
Since Fergus our first King did appear,
Have many hopeful royal princes had,
Who, as heaven pleas'd to bless, were good or bad.
Fergus was the first which we had crown'd,
For learning, and for wisdom high renown'd:
Beyond the verge of Christendom's swift fame,
Did make the world admire his noble name.
A hundred and eleven Kings we have had sincesyne,
' Whereof one of them was a Queen;
Their valour and triumphant victories
Have fill'd the world, and mounts into the skyes:
As Kenneth the Second, that king of victory,
And Gregorius Magnus, whose fame can never dye.
Robertus Brucius, that king of high renown,
King James the Sixth, that united the three crowns;
These victorious princes govern'd well,
But more has been of the contrair strain;
Love sometimes made the gods themselves disguise,
And muffle up their mighty deities,
And virtuous princes of the gods have odds,
When princes goodness doth out-go the gods;
' I'm a foolish man, this is no work of mine,
' It's an operation of the power divine.
Let God alone, for what he hath in hand;
It's saucie, folly and madness to withstand
What his eternal wisdom hath decreed,
Who better knows than we do, what we need.
To him let's pray for his most safe protection,
Him we implore for his most sure direction;
Let his assistance be the seventh King James's guide,
That in the end God may be glorified:
' Let us amendment in our lives express,
' And let our thanks be more, our sins be less.

Thy cusin William Scot in Milsington,
He is a worthy gentleman,
Come of a worthy family,
For he from Whitslade sprung;
Of his brother Todrick I have writ,
And given a true relation,
Of his most worthy pedegree,
Unto the seventh or ninth generation;
Therefore it is needless unto me,
To writ them over again;
For if I please, I could revise
Them to the fifteen generation.
According to my dream, he is the shepherd's swain,
I hope Jason's golden fleece with him shall still remain.

Dedicated to the very worshipful, and much honoured generous gentlemen, Hugh Scot *of* Gallow-shiells, *and* Walter Scot *in* Wauchop.

O! For a quill of that Arabian wing,
   That's hatch't in embers of some kindled fire,
Who to herself, her self doth issue bring,
And, three in one, is young, and dame and sier:
O! that I could to Virgil's vein aspire,
Or Homer's verse, the golden lanuage Greek,
With polish'd phrases, I my lines would tire,
Into the deep of art my muse should seek;
Mean time amongst the vulgar she must throng,
Because she hath no help from my unlearned tongue;
Great is the glory of the noble mind,
Where life and death are equal in respect,
If fates be good or bad, unkind, or kind;
Not proud in freedom nor in thrall deject;
With courage scorning fortune's worst effect,
And spitting in fond envie's cankered face,
True honour thus doth baser thoughts deject;

                                        Esteeming

Esteeming life a slave that serves disgrace,
Foul abject thoughts become the mind that's base,
That deems there is no better life nor this,
Or after death doth fear a worser place,
Where guilt is paid the guardian of a miss;
But let swoln envy swell until she burst,
The noble mind defies her, do her worst;
If Homer's verse in Greek did merit praise,
If Naso in the Latine won the bayes,
If Maro amongst the Romans did excell,
If Tosa in the Testine tongue wrote well;
A souldier that could never lead a pen,
Shows to the eighth or ninth generation,
Although I him enrol, and call him shepherd's swain,
Yet hereby I approve he is a gentleman,
The son of Adam, who was by lot,
The brother of the worthy Colonel Scot,
Who died with honour at Dunbar's fight,
In maintenance of King and country's right:
He was the son, I know it for truth,
Of William Scot, Laird of Whitehaugh;
And William Scot was the eldest son
Of Walter Scot, stil'd of the same;
Walter Scot was Robert's son,
And Robert he was Walter's son:
The first of Whitehaugh that from Borthwick sprung,
That Wat of Whitehaugh was cousin-german
To John of Borthwick, who fasted so long,
' Three sundry times he did perform
' To fast fourty days, I do aver;
Bishop Spotswood, my author is he,
A profound learn'd prelat that would not lie:
When James the First he was Scotland's King,
In the Castle of Edinburgh he incarcer'd him,

And

And would not believe the country says,
That any mortal could fast fourty days;
Bear-bread and water the king allow'd for his meat,
But John Scot refus'd, and would not eat:
' When the fourty days were come and gone,
' He was a great deal lustier than when he began.
Then of the king he did presume,
To beg recommendation to the Pope of Rome,
' Where there he fasted fourty days more,
' And was neither hungry, sick, nor sore:
From Rome he did hastily return,
And arrived in Brittain at London;
Where Henry the Eighth he got notice,
That John Scot had fasted twice fourty days;
The King would not believe he could do such thing,
For which he commanded to incarcerate him;
Fourty days expir'd he said he had no pain,
Than his fast had been but ten hours time:
Here Walter Scot I'll draw near an end,
From John of Borthwick thy fathers did descend;
He was the son of Walter, I have said enough,
Their original is from Buckcleugh.
In the fourscore psalm we read,
That like a flock our God did Joseph lead,
And ev'ry day we do confess almost,
That we have err'd, and stray'd like sheep that's lost,
For oaths, and passing words, and joining hands,
Is like assurance written in the sands,
The silly sheeps-skin turn'd to parchment thin,
Shows that Jason's golden fleece with thee remains.

Dedicated

Past'ral.

Dedicated to the Right Worshipful and truely generous, my well approved good friend, Sir Patrick Scot *of* Long-newton, *appearant of* Ancrum, Knight.

IT'S such a title of preheminence then,
To bear the name of shepherd's swain,
That David who so well his words did frame,
Did call our Great Creator by that name;
Our bless'd Redeemer, God's eternal son,
Whose only merits our salvations won,
He did the harmless name of shepherd take,
For our protection, and his mercie's sake,
Which makes thy rest like those that restless be,
Like one that is pursued, and cannot flie;
Or like the bussie, bussing, bumming bee,
Or like the fruitless naught respected flee,
That cuts the subtile air so swift and fast,
Till in the spidder's webb he's fetter'd fast.
So falling fast asleep, and sleeping in a dream,
Down by that dale which flows with milk and cream,
Thy dearest dame did to thee say,
Francis, Francis, come away;
I wondered when I heard that name begun,
Francis, Francis, that was Adam's son,
And Adam in his time deserv'd no misreport,
He was the son of Gilmanscleugh Robert;
And Robert was a pretty gentleman,
The heir to James, he was his eldest son;
The first of Gilmanscleugh James was then,
Who was the youngest son of Thirlston;
And John of Thirlston I let you know,
Was son to David Scot of Howpaslaw;
And David Scot that worthy man,
Was son to Sir Walter of the same;
For Gilmanscleugh I've said enough,
His first original is from Buckcleugh;

Now of all beasts that ever were or are,
None can for goodness with a sheep compare;
Indeed for bone and burden I must grant,
He's much inferiour to the elephant;
The dromedarie, camel, horse, and ass,
For load and carriage doth the sheep surpass;
Strong Taurus, Eunoch's son, the labouring ox,
The staitly staig, the bobtail crafty fox;
These and all rav'nous beasts of prey must yield,
Unto the sheep, the honour of the field;
Where sheep abounds in Scotland more or less,
There's still a part of Jason's golden fleece.

Dedicated to the worshipful and truely generous gentleman, Robert Scot *laird of* Horsliehill, *son to* William Scot *of* Horsliehill, *who was son to* Robert Scot *portioner and baillie of Hawick, who was son to* William Scot, *who was second son to the* Laird *of* Midgup; Walter Scot *of* Midgup *was grand-child to* Adam Scot *of* Tushilaw, *who was son to the foresaid* David Scot *of* Howpaslaw, *who was son to the first* Sir Walter Scot *of* Howpaslaw; *their original was from* Buckcleugh.

'A simple sheep-skin proves the only ty,
 'And stay whereon a world of men rely,
'Which hold a crew of earth-worms in more awe,
'Then both the tables of the secret law;
For as the rain the ewe doth fructifie,
And ev'ry year a lamb doth multiplie,
So doeth a sheep-skin bound make many breed,
And procreat as seed doth spring from seed,
It's one man's freedom and another's loss,
And like the Pope, it both can bind and loose;
Adam Scot in Delorian I do nominate,
And for thy generation, it cannot be forgot,

Unto

Unto Grass-yard thy brother it is declar'd by me,
Which may serve all that is of one posterity:
And in conclusion this I humbly crave,
That ev'ry one the honesty may have,
That when your frail mortality is past,
Ye may be the good shepherds at the last;
Be not offended at the stile of shepherd's swain,
For Jason's golden fleece is still worthy of coin.

Dedicated to that worthy and valiant souldier, Captain James Scot, *a brigadier in his Majestie's most honourable life-guard, son to* Walter Scot *of* Tushilaw, *who was son to* Robert Scot *of* Tushilaw, *who was son to* Sir Walter Scot *of* Tushilaw, *who was son to* Robert Scot *of* Tushilaw, *who was son to* Adam Scot *of* Tushilaw.

W H O S E former genealogie is already spoken;
The fable of the golden fleece began,
Because sheep did yield such store of gold to men;
For he that hath great store of woolly fleeces,
May, when he pleases, have store of golden pieces;
Honest James Scot of Sheils-wood,
Whose like there is not many,
Whose love and piety doth feed and help so many;
It is no doubt, but these good deeds of his,
Will help to lift his soul to endless bless;
Of his genealogie I will speak no more,
Because his brother Grass-yards is set down before;
I hope Jason's fleece shall never from him flee,
Because he is inclin'd to hospitality.

Dedicated to the worthy and much respected generous gentleman, James Scot *of* Bristo, *Son to* Mr James Scot, *late parson of* Ancrum, *who was son to* John Scot *of* Cachlack-know, *who was son to* Walter Scot *of* Mount-bernger, *who was son to* Robert Scot *of* Mount-bernger, *who was son to* Simon Scot *of* Mount-Bernger, *who was son to* Simon

Simon Scot *of* Dryhop, *who was son to the* Laird *of* Howpaslaw, *whose original is from* Buckcleugh.

MY worthy Cusing, I must to thee commend,
  Him who of his talent surely has made ten,
Like as Joseph did in Ægypt long remain,
Whilst his brether did for food unto him come;
So Gideon privately did live, and made no scroup,
Whilst that his brethren swaggred round about;
But now of Jason's fleece he hath more store,
Than ever his brethren had before;
This Gideon Scot he is a pretty man,
Amongst the rest of worthy shepherds swain,
Of Outer-siderig now he is Laird,
He was son to Robert of Har-wood;
Robert he was a worthy man,
He was son to Walter of Erckletoun;
Walter sprung from that same stock, .
That was call'd John Scot of the New-wark,
And John he was James's son.
My sleeping muse is now layen down,
But when she wakes out of her dream,
The rest of's pedegree I'le explain;
Since he and Jason is so well acquaint,
His golden fleeces he has to him lent.

Dedicated to that generous, and well approved gentleman, James Scot, *Laird of* Bow-hill.

MIRACOLOUS monsters in the British clyme,
  Monsters of nature sprung from putrid Shem,
Sampson that pull'd the gates of Gaza down,
Nor Libian Hercules, whose furious frown,

Would

Would maze strong gyants, tame the lyon's rage,
Were not so strong as gallants of this age;
Why you shall see an up-start cock-brain'd Jack,
Will bear five hundred aikers on his back,
And walk as stoutly, as if it were no load,
And bear it to each place of his abode;
A love-sick woer would a sonnet write,
In praise of her who was his heart's-delight,
Hoping thereby his wished love to win,
And to obtain it, thus he did begin.

 Star of the earth, and empress of my soul,
Thy love and life, that doth my thoughts controul,
Sole queen of my affections and desire,
That like to Ætna sets my heart on fire,
Thy golden locks resembling Titan's amber,
Most fit to grace some mighty monarch's chamber:
Thine eyes eclipsing Titan in his rising,
Thy face surpassing nature's best devising,
Thy lips evaporate most sweet perfumes,
Thy voice the musick of the sphers assumes;
Perfections wound more than loves shaft and bow,
Thy red the rose doth shame, thy white the snow,
Thou world's wonder, nature's clearest feuel,
Stain not thy vertues with thy being cruel;
Besides it is an easie thing to prove,
It is a sovereign remedy for love,
As suppose your thoughts at hourly strife,
Half mad, and almost weary of your life:
All for the love of some fair female creature,
And that you are intangled with her feature;
' That you are glad, and sad, and mad, and tame,
' Seeming to burn in frost, and frieze in flame;
' In one breath, singing, laughing, weeping,
' Dream as you walk, and waking in your sleeping,

Accounting hours for years, and months for ages,
Till you enjoy her that your heart engages,
And she hath sent you answers long before,
That her intent is not to be your whore;
And you, for your part, mean upon your life,
Ne're while you live to take her to your wife;
The west-border seed, it is not fit for you,
You may procure better than there doth grow;
Thou art the brother by thy place unto a lovely swain,
The son of that renowned squire, John Scot of Rennal-burn
Thy father Robert yet survives
Thy guid-sir was by the Napiers slain,
Thy grand-sir the first laird of Bow-hill,
Was son to John Scot of Thirlston.
A worthy squire John Scot of Reunal-burn,
He was the son of that Sir John Scot,
Whom the muses lov'd, and hovered at his gate.
And Sir John was son of that learned man,
Mr Arthur Scot who was stil'd of New-burgh than;
And Mr Arthur was brave Simon's son,
He who was tutor to the pupils of Thirlston;
And John of Thirlston that brave fellow,
Was son to David Scot of Howpaslaw,
And David was the first Sir Walter's son:
So, James, thy genealogy I have done,
And spoken nothing but the very truth,
Thy original is from Buckcleugh;
Since fates allow the harmless beasts such store,
I hope of Jason's fleece thou shalt have more and more.

Dedicated to the honourable and truly noble, Sir William Elliot *of* Stobs, *Knight and Baronet.*

IT's not in expectation of reward,
   That I this book into your hands do render,

But in my humble duty in regard,
That I am bound my dayly thanks to render;
If my verse be defective, and my accent rude,
My stile be harsh, and my learning slender,
I am defended against a multitude,
If that your patronage be but my defender.
This to avoid hell's-hatcht ingratitude,
My duteous love, my lines and life shall be,
To you devoted, ever to conclude;
May you, and your most vertuous Lady see
Long happy days, in honour still encreasing,
And after death true honour never ceasing.

 Your Worship's parents were so well known by me,
That I'm bold to show them to the fourth degree,
These worthy families I must needs commend,
From whom Sir William Elliot of Stobs did descend:
I here set down the number what they are,
And then I'le nominate them in particular.
Thy thirty ancestors I would have men to ken,
Thy eight great grandsirs, and thy eight great grandames,
Thy grandsirs and grandames eight, that makes twenty four,
Thy goodsirs and goodames four, with father and mother;
Thy thirty ancestors I have set down,
And thou thyself makes thirty and one;
This true account from whence your Worship sprung,
Is just to the fourth generation of your kin:
Thy first great grandsir and grandam, it's of truth,
Was Elliot of Lariston, and Scot of Buckcleugh;
To thy second great grandsir and grandam now I trot,
They were Scot of Hardin, and Scot of Dryhop;
Thy third great grandsir and grandam to their name,
Was Douglas of Cavers, and a sister of Cranston;
Thy fourth great grandsir to his name,
Was Douglas the Laird of Whittinghame;

I am not certain, yet have heard some mean,
He was married to Hepburn a daughter of Waughton;
Thy fifth great grandsir to whom I flee,
Was Sir John Cranston, and Ramsay of Dalhousie;
Thy sixth great grandsir and grandam I set down,
Was Cranston of Moriston, and Cockburn of Lanton;
Thy seventh great grandsir and grandam I reveal,
Was Lord Seton of Seton and Maxwel of Maxwel;
Thy eight great grandsir and grandam no less,
Then Earl Bothwell and Dowglas sister to the Earl Angus.
   Now to the first grandsir and grandam I come,
Elliot of Stobs, and Scot of Hardin;
To the second grandsir and grandam now I run,
Sir William of Cavers, and Dowglas of Whittinghame;
Thy third grandsir and grandam I must proclaim,
Was William Lord Cranston, and Sarah daughter to Sir John;
Thy fourth grandsir was the Lord Coldinghame.
Now to thy first goodsir I do rehearse,
Which was Elliot of Stobs and Dowglas of Cavers,
Thy other goodsir and goodam of much renown,
Was Mr of Cranston, and daughter to Lord Coldinghame,
Thy father and mother who still lives by fame,
Sir Gilbert of Stobs, and sister to Lord Cranston;
Although I cannot write, yet I have spent my breath,
In dilating thy descent from good King James the Fifth.
Earl Bothwel thy great grandsir,
Was a valiant man,
He was King James the Fifth
His own natural-son.
   And now I humbly crave your worthiness excuse,
For the boldness of my unlearned muse,
That hath presumed so high a pitch to flee,
In praise of virtue and gentilitie;

I know this task is fit for learned men,
For Homer, Ovid, or for Virgil's pen;
Boldly to write true honour's worthiness,
Whilst better muses pleased to hold their peace;
And this much to the world my verse proclaims,
That neither gain nor flattery are my ends;
But love and duty to your familie
Has caus'd my muse these lines to publish'd be:
And therefore I intreat your generous heart,
To accept my duty and pardon my neglects,
Bear with my weakness, wink at my defects,
Good purposes do merit good effects.
Poor earthen vessels may hold precious wine,
And I presume that in this book of mine,
In many places ye shall something find,
To please its noble well affected mind;
And for excuse, my muse doth humbly plead,
That ye'll forbear to judge before ye read.

    The Persians, Egyptians, and the Israelites,
And raging Razin, King of Aramites,
Then the Assyrians twice, and then again
The Egyptians over-run them all amain.
Then the Chaldeans, and once more they came,
Egyptian Ptolomey, who them overcame;
Then Pompey next king, Herod last of all,
Vespasian was their universal fall
As in Assyria monarchy began,
They lost it to the warlike Persian;
Of Nimrod's race a race of kings descended,
Till in Astiages his stock was ended;
For Cyrus into Persia did translate
The Assyrian soveraign monarchizing state;
Then after many bloody bruising arms,
The Persian yielded to the Greeks alarms:

But smoak-like Grecian glory lasted not,
Before 'twas ripe it did untimely rot:
The world's commander, Alexander, died,
And his successors did the world divide;
From one great monarch in a moment springs
Confusion, Hydra-like, from self-made kings;
Till they all wearied, slaughtered and forlorn,
Had all the earth dismember'd, rent and torn;
The Romans took advantage of their fall,
And over-ran, captiv'd, and conquer'd all:
Thus, as one nail another out doth drive,
The Persians the Assyrians did deprive;
The Grecians then the Persian pride did tame,
The Romans then the Grecians overcame;
Whilst like a vapour all the world was tost,
And kingdoms were transferr'd from coast to coast;
And still the Jews in scatter'd multitudes,
Deliver'd were to sundry servitudes,
Chang'd, given, bought, and sold from land to land,
Where they not understood, nor understand,
To every monarchy they were made slaves,
Egypt, Aram, Chaldea, them outbraves,
Assyria, Persia, Grecia, lastly Rome,
Invaded them by heavens just angry doom;
Four ages did the sons of Heber pass,
Before their final dissolution was;
Their first age, aged patriarchs did guide,
The second reverend judges did decide;
The third by kings, nought, good, bad, worse and worst,
The fourth by prophets, who them blest or curst,
As their dread God commanded or forbid,
To curse or bless, even so the prophets did.

    Good reader, I have writ these lines to let thee know withall,
What desolations did in former ages fall,

And here within sixscore of year,
By many families it doth appear,
Who were men of note, and their substance did abound.
Yet to great servitude their children came;
But yet I think men should not fret,
' For a suspension never pays no debt;
For if a man according to the laws,
He be captivat for an onerous cause,
And then from bondage he again return,
This is no act of credit left by him.
In histories its often read,
That kings sons have been tradesmen bred;
Crispin and Crispianus the English sing,
Was son to Braenus the British King,
Of such a change men they may admire,
' From a crown to become a cordiner;
If his son's son did live to be a man,
And if that he might rightly play his game,
Durst any poultry pismee call him down,
' By exclamation to be a sutor's son.
These idle questionists, and these schismaticks,
I hold no better than rank hereticks;
But this I think not well when honest hearts,
Shall have this undervaluing name without deserts;
If every hair upon the heads of men
Were quills, and every quill a pen,
Were earth to paper turn'd, and seas to ink,
And all the world were writers, yet I think
They could not write enough of mischief's strain,
Calumnious boasters, bloody tongued men.
Of Persians, Pagans, Asians, or Rome,
' I need not write, there's division enough at home.
   For the Elliots brave and worthy men,
Have been as much oppress'd as any name I ken,

For in my own time I have seen so much odds,
No Elliot enjoyed any heritage, but Dunlibire, Fanash, and Stobs;
Stobs being *sine qua non*, and obedient to the truth,
A beloved sister-son to the family of Buckcleugh:
Yet in the border-side the Elliots did remain,
Since King Robert the First, they with him from Angus came.
The town of Elliot was their antiquitie,
Which stands in Angus in the foot of Glenshie;
With brave King Robert the Bruce they hither came,
Which is three hundred and eighty years agone;
In west Tiviotdale these gentlemen did dwell,
They were twelve great families, I heard my good-sir tell;
Their chief was then a baron of renown,
Designed Reid-heugh, which is now call'd Lariston;
Stobs and Dunlibyre is of the antient kind,
Cobshaw, Brugh, Prickinhaugh, and Gorinberrie's gone,
Yet there's more Elliots by other stiles that supplies their room;
Erckletoun it was long out of the Elliots name,
But now it is return'd to the self same again;
Elliot of Bewlies, some say, he's not a gentleman;
But I protest they do him wrong to his ninth generation;
What if a man have sons three,
Procreat and born from one belly,
Can one of them be a gentleman,
And another be a peasant's son?
' He neither descends from kill nor mill,
He's sprung from the Laird of Horsliehill,
Thereof his grandsir was a younger brother-son,
Though he was servant to the Laird of Hardin;
Hardin the foresaid William did so much esteem,
That he in marriage his natural daughter did gain,
And betwixt them two was procreat, I must reveal,
That Robert Elliot that lived in Borthwick-sheill;
And Robert Elliot married a gentle dame,
Hately from the family of Mellarstain,

Betwixt

Betwixt them two was procreat sure,
Good Thomas Elliot in Borthwick-sheils,
That much reliev'd the poor;
And Thomas Elliot married then,
The daughter of the laird chamberlain Newton,
And procreat betwixt them be
William Elliot of Bewlie;
William Elliot of Bewlie, ye understand the man,
He's married with the sister of Scot of Sinton,
' Who him calumniats with a mis-report,
' I'le say he is a liar in his throat;
For Romulus that builded Rome,
Was nurs'd upon a bear, yet was a prince's son;
The father of the faithful, Abram, Abel and Lot,
Were shepherds in there time, yet types and patriarchs;
The Schythian shepherd, a conqueror compleat,
Tammerlane the Great, yet he attended sheep;
He is but *mala fama* whatever be his coyn,
That says that Bewlie is not a gentleman:
Walter of Erckleton these mis-reports may clear,
For he was called nothing but shepherd fourty year;
And yet he is the just and very man,
Whose goodsir and grandsir was Lairds of Erckleton;
Even though Horsliehill were to sell at this time,
And William Elliot were he that should it gain,
It were but a suspension he had underline,
Being truely descended from that self same kind;
And though that his grandsir was a servant man,
For the want of means to the Laird of Hardin,
And he by his service and good husbandry,
Had purchased means might set Horsliehill free;
But being not to sell, he purchas'd other lands,
' Doth that make out that he's not a gentleman?
The Elliots of the Yare they are of that same kind,
And the Elliots of Selkirk they are of the same,

If James Elliot, late of Bridgeheugh, be a gentleman,
Then William Elliot of Bewlie must needs be one;
For their grandsirs were two brother-sons,
Though in occupation there was defference,
The one a magistrat in Selkirk town,
The other kept the sheep upon the Doun;
The one did live by polling of the poor,
Being magistrat was counted great honour;
The other was a shepherd's swain, and reliev'd the poor that came,
With bed and board, though but a servant man.
Sixty years ago I have both heard and seen,
And knew that Robert was the Laird of Hardin's man;
Yet he was the poors reliefs,
For he fed and clad them both with flesh and fleece;
But for the magistrat few poor he did relieve,
He was still ready to take, but never to give:
' Sir Baillie, if't please your Worship,
Was the word of every one;
The other was Will or Hab,
Yet both from brethren came;
Their foresaid marriages they are set down by me,
To be a truth I will affirm, and that they are no ly;
I have both eat and drunk, and merry with them been,
All of them except the first William,
Which my father knew, and that very well,
To be of the family of these of Horsliehill;
And since Horsliehill was thy fore-father's stile,
Bewlie it hath been the same for a pretty while:
And I still do wish that stile do remain,
With thee and with thine, till the period of time:
Yet pardon my lines, though they be out of frame,
For I could never any write but the letters of my name;

            And

And although that they be not pleasant to the view,
Yet they are both honest, modest, chaste, and true;
And though Jason fetch'd his golden fleece from Greece,
Thy fleece in Scotland it is many poors relief.

Dedicated to the very honourable, and much respected generous Gentleman, the Laird of Lariston.

COULD my unpractis'd pen advance thy name,
Thou should be mounted on the wings of fame,
Thy ancestors they were of good renown,
They being all the lairds of Lariston;
Into thy hands I do commit the sum
Of Walter Elliot of Erckleton,
By Maxwel's rage out of their hands it got,
And was possess'd by Cunninghame and Scot;
Now Providence has brought it back again,
To the lineal heir of Elliot's kind;
For Walter Elliot he was Adam's son,
And Adam's goodsir was Laird of Erckleton;
Though they were suspended for an age or twain,
The lands return'd to Elliot of Muckildine;
He is the Laird of Erckleton's brother,
And Janet Scot she is Muckildine's mother,
A worthy wife she of long time hath been,
And hath fill'd many poor and hungry womb;
She is my friend, therefore I do her ken,
She's daughter to John Scot, call'd of Rennalburn,
An honest gentleman, he was known well enough,
In Esdail-muir, he was baillie to Buckcleugh,
' Who was son to John Scot, an able lad,
' Who then was called Jocky ill to had;
His father also he was called John,
He was natural son to Scot of Thirlston,

He

He was natural brother in the while
To Thirlston Newburgh and Bowhill,
Gilmansclough, Hundelshope, and Kirkhope,
Were all brethren to the said John Scot;
These seven brethren were stout valiant men,
They would not be afraid for other ten;
No more of Muckildine since Adam is deceast,
Who left them store like Jason's golden fleece.

Dedicated to the very worthy and valorous gentleman, William Elliot *of* Dunlibire, *Esquire.*

I Humbly now, according to my dream,
  Present to you the young Laird of Erckleton,
From 's goodsir and grandsir that land was reft and riven,
Before they purchas'd coyn to buy it back again;
And now 'tis their own, I wish they may 't enjoy,
From Envy's cauker, better than Helen did Troy;
That Trojan and that Greek that fought in Sama sand,
Achilles gain'd the day, and did Hector command;
Troy's fruitful queen did many children bear,
So brave, heroick, and so stout a crew,
Who all in noble actions did accrue,
When age had made their parents bald and bare,
They made their dauntless courage to appear,
Amidst the throngs of danger and debate,
But blood on blood their fury could not fate:
In former times the South may understand,
Many gallants losed all their land,
Through blood and want of government,
Which to this time successors may repent;
They were not like these Arcadians in Greece,
That rejoyc'd in Jason's golden fleece.

Dedicated

Dedicated to that worthy and generous gentleman, Robert Elliot Laird *of* Midliemill.

SIR, in my sleep I was much troubled,
And dream'd of Henry Elliot of Harewood,
'Mongst many more that I thought I saw,
And knowing he was your father in law,
Therefore my weak judgement thought it fit,
Those lines to you that I should dedicat;
Knowing him to be a worthy man,
And much honour'd by your generation;
Though all in one you now joined be,
Yet ye're a peer grew higher on the tree;
For I believe there is so much odds,
Few Elliots compared with the house of Stobs;
For Heav'n's high hand where he doth please to bless,
Makes trees, or men, fruitful, or fruitless;
In sundrie uses trees do serve mens turn,
To build, adorn, to feed, or else to burn;
This is mens state in all degrees like theirs,
Some are got to the top of honour's stairs,
Securely sleeping on opinion's pillow,
Yet is as fruitless as the fruitless willow,
And fill up room, like worthless trees in woods,
Whose goodness consists all in ill-got goods;
He like a cedar makes a goodly show,
But now good fruit will from his greatness grow,
Untill he die, and from his goods depart,
And then gives all away in the spight of his heart;
' Then shall his friends with mourning cloaths be clad,
' The inside merry, and the outside sad;
He thinks his life angelical, because
Among the angels he his time doth pass;
And with his nobles he ordaineth laws,
That base extortion shall not be a crime;
He marks how kingdoms, provinces, and towns,
Are over-ruled by his cursed crowns,

But if he note his angels what to be,
Not heavenly, nor these from heaven that fell,
But they are in a third and worse degree,
Damn'd sensless monsters, even that are of hell,
They cannot hear, feel, taste, hear, or smell,
A thousand times being told yet cannot tell;
They're lock'd and barr'd, and bolted up in thrall,
Which shews their nature not angelical;
Thy industrious loyalty doth daily tell,
Thou aims at honour and thou levels well,
And with your trusty service shot compleat,
That in the end you shure will hit the whyte;
Thus thy industries doth let the world ken,
That Jason's golden fleece with thee shall still remain.

Dedicated to that worthy and well approved gentleman, John Elliot, *brother to* Sir William Elliot *of* Stobs.

GOOD Sir, if fortune frown or smile, thou art content,
Thou bears a heart that is still ready bent;
God is thy captain, thy defence and hold,
Through faith in him thou art still armed bold;
To thank John Elliot I humbly thee desire,
He dwells in Unthank, he's brother to Dunlibire:
When kind kissing Phoebus was gone to her rest,
In a winter's night in a most furious blast,
I driving beasts because I wanted fodder,
I did assault his house into tempestuous weather;
For god Æolus blew, and Boreas did assist,
And Neptune's watery planets he broke in betwixt,
The snow being deep, the snow tempestuous ill,
I was five days in driving twenty mile;
In great distress into his house I came,
He with his wife made me kindly welcome,

With

With bed and board, good brandie and good ale,
Which might have serv'd the best in Tiviotdale.
I wish John Elliot never want such fleeces,
Which yearly may bring in ten thousand golden pieces.

Dedicated to that much renowned generous gentleman, William Elliot, *uncle to* Sir William Elliot *of* Stobs.

M OST worthy Sir, I hope I do no wrong,
In dedicating to you one of my shepherd's swains;
Take not a shepherd swain to be a vulgar name,
For kings and emperors have gloried in the same;
Therefore no shepherd swain my muse shall e're deride,
And far less William Elliot the good Laird of Swoonside,
Since thou art worthy and a lovely one,
Not like envy, all consum'd to skin and bone.
Sir, I do declare what labour thou hast spent,
Was neither to honour nor vertue's detriment;
And thrice worthy Sir, thy vertues do proclaim,
How honour's noble mark it is still thy aim,
And when thou the head-strong Taurus soon forsakes,
And to his summering progress thou haste makes,
Then shall the earth's celestial light afford,
And in sad darkness clad the ample globe;
Since I was born, when wit was out of town,
That's the reason that I have so little of my own;
Pardon me, I cannot write, and very little read,
Or else in thy worthy praise, I further would proceed;
As for Swoonside, I wish his golden fleece
May shine as bright as Jason's did in Greece.

Dedicated to that vertuous and well approven gentleman, Mr Gavin Elliot, *uncle to* Sir William Elliot *of* Stobs.

M OST worthy Sir, according to my dream,
I speak of shepherds, and of shepherd's swain:

Into

Into your gentle hands, Sir, I do commit,
John Elliot, the Laird of Thorilshope;
And Sir, I do hope that ye'l not disallow,
That I have been so bold as dedicat him to you;
For a man must more than human wit possess,
To escape the baits and snares of wickedness:
The artist of the scripture can dispute the same,
That one would deem him a religious man;
Since that God gave life to herbs, and plants, and trees,
A beast hath sense, and life, moves, feels, and sees;
For if they wanted life, how could they then grow,
And in some sort, do both good and evil know;
But man he is before all creatures in degrees,
God, life, sense, and reason, he unto him gives;
And least that these blessings should be transitory,
He gave him life and sense, reason, grace, and glory;
So I hope Thorilshope shall keep his golden fleece,
As glorious as Jason did his in Greece.

Dedicated to that worthy and compleat gentleman, Robert Elliot *appearant of* Dunlibire.

MOST worthy Sir, I do upon the wings of fame,
 Dedicat to you one of your worthy name,
John Elliot, he who's call'd a valiant lad,
He's brother to Henry Elliot of Harewood;
It was into my dream he did appear to me,
For I into the ale-house did him never see;
In Jason's golden fleece it's said he doth abound,
And now he is of late a person much renown'd,
Therefore I him consecrat to thee,
And with happiness to you, and your posterity,
Wishing to him when he his sheep doth shear,
They may improve their fleece four times a year,

For that man that hath store of wool, and woolly fleeces,
May when he please, have store of gold and golden pieces.

Dedicated to that valorous and compleat young gentleman, Robert Elliot *appearant of* Lariston.

SIR, these lines unto your hand I send,
 Wishing your worship will but them commend,
And begs that you'l not be a gast,
For nominating some first that should be last;
Therefore, good Sir, I hope you will pardon give,
And oblige your humble servant while he lives;
This I lay open to your Worship's view,
And Simon Elliot of Tarras, I dedicat to you;
For summer-fruit it is pleasant to eat,
But winter it will a long time keep;
Although the hills of Tarras they be black
Yet in his golden fleece there is no lack;
Black moisty fleeces when they are well scour'd,
Unto the owners yield good, clear, and current gold.
Pure Spanish gold it's very fine,
But of wool our merchants makes more gain;
Through Christendom your woolly fleeces,
Are still compar'd to golden pieces;
So he that is a shepherd's swain,
Can be no less than a gentleman:
Monarchs and kings, royal majesty,
Were shepherd's swains in Arcadie.

Dedicated to the young and very hopeful gentleman, Gilbert Elliot, *son to* Sir William Elliot *of* Stobs, *Knight Baronet.*

IF Homer's verse in Greek did merit praise,
 If Nason in the Latin tongue wan bayes,
If Maro 'mongst the Romans did excel,
If Tasso in the Tuscian tongue spoke well:

Sweet Sir, pardon him that's so much unperfect,
In Scots can scarcely read, and never could yet write;
If my poor shallow brain could but advance your name,
Ye shall be mounted high upon the wings of fame;
And if that my poor thoughts had strength to enterprize,
I would advance your name as far as Titan's rise,
And that shepherd swain that I do simulize,
Is Robert Elliot that dwells in the Dewslies:
Be not offended at the name of shepherd swain,
For formerly that name was noblemen;
And as Jason fetcht his golden fleece from Greece,
I wish that Robert Elliot his fleeces may increase.

Dedicated to the very honourable, and right worshipful generous gentleman, John Hoppringil, Laird *of* Torsonce.

IF the value of offerings are always to be equal to the grandeur of the persons to whom they are represented, I should not dare to make this bold address; but the greatness of my devotion, that hath no other way to manifest itself at present, will, I hope, make amends for the means of this, and persuade your Worship to condescend to the acceptance of this poor expression of my respects; if these treatises may be so happy, as to give unto your Worship some satisfaction and recreation in the perusal of them, I shall attain unto the advantage, which is chiefly aimed at by this dedication,

Your Worship's most obedient, most humble
and faithful servant,
WALTER SCOT.

MOST worthy Sir, ye know this well by me,
   That the love of brandie made my self merrie,
For when the high born bastard of the thundring Jove,
When mens inventions are of wit most hollow,
He with his sprightful juice their spirits doth move,
To the harmonious musick of Apollo,

' And

' And in a word, I would have all men know it,
' He must drink brandy that means to be a poet ;
I understand, or know no foreign tongue,
But their translations I do much admire,
Much art, much pains, much study it doth require,
And at the least regard should be their hyre ;
When Adam was in Paradice first placed,
And with the rule of mortal things was graced,
Then roses, pinks, and fragrant gilly-flowers,
Adorn'd and deckt forth Eden's blessed bowers ;
Love is a dying life, and living death ;
A vapour shaddow, a bubble, and a breath,
An idle bable, and a poultry toy,
Whose greatest patron is a blinded boy ;
But pardon love, my judgement is unjust,
For what I speak of love, I mean'd of lust ;
' Bess she dislikes the surplice and the cap,
' And calls them idle vestments of the Pope ;
' And Mistress Maud would go to church right fain.
' But that the corner cap makes her refrain ;
' And Madam Idle is offended deep,
' The preacher speaks so loud she cannot sleep ;
Lo thus the devil sowes contentions seed,
Whence sects, and schisms, and heresies do breed ;
Since Providence has given you wit in store,
Live as your worthy fathers did live you before.
By night I in a vision did dream,
That four and twenty shepherds I had seen,
Whereof John Andison was one ;
A shepherd swain that dwells in Thirleston ;
A civil person, and one that is true,
And therefore I dedicat him to you ;
I hope the name of shepherd ye'l not despise it,
Since kings and princes hath it enterprized,

Besides

Besides the learned poets of all times,
Have chanted out their praises in pleasant rymes,
The harmless lives of rural shepherd swains,
And beauteous shepherdesses on the plains ;
They have recorded most delightfully,
Their love, their fortune, and felicity ;
And sure if in this low terrestrial round,
Plain honest happiness is to be found,
It with the shepherd is remaining still,
Because they have least power to do ill ;
And whilst they on the feeding flocks attend,
They have the least occasion to offend ;
I wish God bless the shepherds and their fleeces,
And then I hope they'l ne're want golden pieces.

Dedicated to the very honourable, and right worshipful generous gentleman, John Riddel *of* Haining, *Sherif-principal of the Sherifdom of Selkirk, and Provost of that Burgh-Royal.*

I Humbly wish peace, truth, and constancy,
  Remain with you and your worthy family ;
That sailor gains renown that well does know,
To gain his point either at ebb or flow,
When Boreas' dust doeth drive thee from the land,
Then Æolus' blasts puts thee in Neptun's hand ;
To wonder and admire is all one thing,
As synonymies the word betake ;
But if a double meaning from them come,
For double sense your judgement then must look ;
As once a man all foul'd with dirt and myre,
Fell down and wondered not, but did admire ;
To you whose ears, and eyes have heard and seen,
This little pamphlet, and can judge between,

That

That which is good, tolerable, or ill,
May be with artless nature wanting skill:
Have I writ ought that may your hearts content,
My muse hath then accomplisht her intent,
Your favour can preserve me, but your frown
My poor intentions in oblivion drown;
With tolerable friendship let me crave,
You will not seek to spill what you may save.
The Asp that quakes with sun,
He doth me much deride,
' The Webster and the Smith,
' They shake their brainless head,
And says, my education, or my state,
Doth make my verse esteem'd at lower rate:
To such as those, this answer I do send,
And bid them mend before they discommend,
Their envy unto me will favours prove.
The hatred of fools breeds wise mens love;
My muse is jocund, that her labours merits
To be malign'd and scorn'd by envyous carriage.
This humbly I beg pardon of the best,
Which being granted, Sir, a reverence for the rest:
Why should they vex in their malicious brain,
For I have done no wrong to you nor them;
A greedy wretch did on the scripture look,
Found it recorded in the sacred book,
How such a man with God should sure prevail,
Who clad the naked, and visited them in joal,
And there he found how he had long mistaken,
And oftentimes had made the cloathed naked;
In stead of visiting the opprest in moans,
He had consum'd them to the very bones;
Yet one day he at leisure would repent,
But sudden death repentance did prevent;

Then he was dead, and laid into his tomb,
In hopes repentance from purgatory come;
There lay the Stuart of the valiant ten,
Who, whilst on life his beloved life remain'd;
Apollo's daughter, and the heirs of Jove,
The memorable bounty did approve;
His life was life to Statius, and his death,
Bereaved the muses of celestial breath;
Had Phœbus fir'd him from the lofty skies,
That Phenix-like another might arise,
From out of his odoriferous sacred embers,
His loved life the country still remembers;
Amongst a million there is hardly any,
That like yourself, so well can govern many.
Now I think well I will reveal,
My dream I must proclaim,
And dedicat unto your hands, my honest shepherd's swain,
That merrily upon the plain doth sing with joking lees,
His shepherdess she does not miss to crown his head with bayes;
Love, bounty, valour, charity with shepherds did remain,
It's Kings and Emperors liberty to be a shepherd's swain,
In meadows green where flowers do spring,
There they do feed their flocks,
Sometimes on mountains and on hills,
Sometimes amongst the rocks;
Their worthy generosity to love is a strong fort,
With triumph doth that trumpet sound,
At the shepherd swain's port,
The best of men are shepherd swains,
As I before design'd,
The eastern-coasts did brag and boast,
Of their brave shepherd's swain:

George

Post'ral.

George Currors then a shepherd swain,
That gains both corn and store,
And doth afford both bed and board,
And much relieves the poor;
In Hart-wood-myres his barns and byres,
And shepherds do remain,
His flocks proceed, and swiftly feed
Upon the morning dew;
And when bright Phœbus takes her coach,
They are in Haining's view,
Of that shepherd's truth I cannot dyte enough,
But now I'm run ashore;
For shepherds swains, their ewes and lambs,
I have spoken much before;
Though Jason fetcht his fleece from Greece,
And was call'd the golden swain,
George Curror that dwells in Hart-wood-myres,
For wool more guilt doth gain,

Dedicated to the learned and well approved generous gentleman, Andrew Plummer, Laird *of* Middlestead.

Most Worthy Sir, Sedition and Commonwealth was intimated by two lobsters, fighting one with another; the land-lobster is a great enemy to the serpents and snakes; therefore the Egyptian priests did put it to signify a temperate man, who suppresseth his lusts and wicked affections, that are the most dangerous serpents unto his soul.

THIS pamphlet I send to your view,
   Is to let your Worship ken,
It's known to be the first issue
Of my dull idle brain;
It's known as yet, I could ne're write,
My reading is but small,
For refuge, I flee to your hands,
In hopes you'l warrand all:

Shepherds

Shepherds I thought were three times eight,
Appear'd into my dream,
Wherefore one to you I dedicat,
A civil honest man;
He in Analshope doth dwell,
His name's Michael Andison;
That shepherd swain will no man wrong,
In religion he is strong;
The foulest fiends assume the fairest forms,
The fairest fields doth feed the foulest toad,
The sea at calmest most subject is to storms,
In chosiest fruit the canker makes abode;
So in the shop of all believing trust,
Lyes toads invenom'd treason couched fast,
Till like a storm his toothless thoughts outburst,
Who canker-like had lyen in trust's repose;
For as the fire within the flint's confin'd,
In deepest ocean still unquench'd remains;
Even so the false, though truest seeming mind,
Despight of truth the treason still retains,
Yet maugure treason, truth deserveth trust,
And trust survives when treason dies accurst:
Since Micheal Andison hath great store of woolen fleece,
I wish they more abound than Jason's did in Greece.

Dedicated to that valiant and generous gentleman, James Gladstains *of that ilk*, Laird *of* Cocklaw.

MOST worthy Sir, I send into your view,
    This little pamphlet, most of it is true;
According to my dream, I yet commend,
I know no foolish man can you offend;
Of four and twenty shepherds I did dream,
Whereof James Grieve in Commonside was one,

An

An honest man you know it sure,
And one that doth relieve the poor;
Your generous noble sp'rit, as I do understand,
Emboldens me to dedicat him to your hand;
He that may hunt on every inclosed ground,
A park of's own he needeth not to found;
The staitly staig when he his horns hath shed,
In sullen sadness he deplores his loss;
But when a wife cornuts her husband's head,
His gains in horns he holds an extream cross;
' The staig of lossing, doth his loss complain,
' The man by gaining doth lament his gain:
Thus whether horns he either loss or found,
They both the loser and the winner wound.
Hunting is pleasant, but yet wearisome,
To him that can no venison obtain;
Though worthy swain chuse in Diana's stream,
Amongst the sisters nine, and pick out one of them,
Wit, courage, valour, stature, and state,
Remain with thee, don't fear a horned pate:
Now, good James Grieve, I wish thy flocks increase,
That thou may chant and sing, and still keep Jason's fleece.

Dedicated to the very worthy and much respected generous gentleman,
  Robert Langlands *of that Ilk.*

WHEN fond imaginary dreams do ring,
  In formless forms in mens molested brain,
On such a time, I sleeping in my bed,
An unnaccustom'd dream came in my head;
I thought four and twenty to me came,
All gentlemen and shepherds swain,
Whereof James Grieve Lenup he was one,
Which I have dedicated unto your worship's hand;

You know him well to be an honest man,
And is a just and harmless shepherd swain;
His fleece doth clothe the naked, that there's none deny,
His food relieves the needy, as they pass him by,
The orphan, widow, and the indigent,
For bed and board from him have supplement.
These shepherd swains, as I do understand,
Relieves more poor, nor all the lairds of the land;
Their butter, cheese, their milk, their whey,
Their flesh and wool, they part continually,
That I dare say, were their not such men,
Five thousand in the year would starve and pine:
God bless their substance, that helps the poor folks messes,
And send them store of wool to bring them golden pieces.

Dedicated to the worthy and much respected gentleman, Francis Gladstains *of* Whitlaw.

MOST worthy Sir, do not disdain,
That I my dream so oft explain;
Unto your hands I do it commit,
The issue of barren wit;
A great deal more from me might appear,
Within this seventy and two year,
But what is past I cannot now recall,
I hope ye'l think this makes amends for all:
I never was at school, I cannot write,
Pardon my lines, though they be unperfyte;
The best of gallants indeed may controul,
A wise man will ever countenance a fool,
Although in wrong he will not bear him up,
Yet he will laugh at his foolish fate;
The four and twenty of my dream,
William Grieve of Common-side was one,

Which I have dedicat to you,
He is an honest man and true;
A worthy shepherd's swain, who lives upon his store,
And relieves the poor and needy, as I have said before.
I wish his golden fleece with him may still remain,
While I fetch Jason's fleece from Greece into Scotland.

Dedicated to the generous, and much respected gentleman, Walter Scot *of* Burn-foot.

MOST worty Sir, according to my dream,
   Into this pamphlet remains to be seen,
I hope your goodness will allow,
That I dedicat Walter Grieve to you;
He is a true and honest man,
He's both your neighbour, and shepherd's swain;
One dedication might have serv'd for all,
What I have said before, to mention it again,
It is a needless labour, and puts the writer to more pain;
I wish ye miekle joy of all your golden pieces,
And like to Walter Grieve, with increase of his fleeces.

Dedicated to his worthy, and well respected good friend, Francis Scot, *brother-german to the laird of* Burn-foot *in* Ail.

SIR, this pamphlet to your hands I send,
   In hopes that ye will it commend;
For pens ye know I can use none,
I can hardly read the catechism;
Yet four and twenty shepherds,
I saw into my dream,
Whereof good Thomas Anderson,
In Howfoord he was one;

Seeing ye are a gentleman, and my friend,
I have dedicate him into your hand:
When Jupiter the son of Saturn
Had put his father to the flight,
The Empire of the world he did divide then,
Betwixt himself and his brother Neptune;
Neptune set Pluto for to dwell in Hell,
Amongst the priests, where still they do rebel;
The sacred records they do demonstrate,
The idols which the Israelites did prostrate,
So do we find into the present time,
That there are priests of every kind,
Kings, prophets, priests, by all were shepherds swains,
And did attend all kind of sheep,
Both weathers, ewes and lambs:
For Thomas Anderson I wish his flocks may still abound,
If Jason lost his golden fleece, I'm sure he has it found.

Dedicated to the worshipful and very much respected and generous gentleman, Henry Forrester *of* Stonegirthside, *in the kingdom of* England, *justice of peace and coram in the said kingdom, in the reign of King* Charles *the Second.*

COME, Pamphlet, take thy wings, flee from my hand,
Arrive in England, in the county of Cumberland,
There stands a house, and that a worthy one,
By Kersup-foot in the eye of the sun;
A stately building, all of plain hew'n stone,
All built within this year or twain,
All Cumberland, except castle and abbay,
Such another house in prospect you'll not see;
Unto that English squire I dedicat
Honest John Robertson, he was born in the Flat;
His father was an English man,
Francis Robson kept good order.

There

There was no English compar'd with him,
Seven mile within the border;
Justice Forrester an English Squire,
And John Robson a Scot,
Yet it is scarce a mile betwixt,
Where they were born and got;
It's true John Robson is
A comrade good enough,
And for house-keeping he excels,
He dwells in Cauterscleugh,
White-bread and salt-beef,
Good mutton and old cheese,
As I was riding by,
He did my hunger ease,
He feasted me in May, as I had been an Earl,
With capon and good lamb, brandie and good ale;
And for his father Francis,
I knew him well enough
To be a gentleman, store-master
To Walter Earl of Buckcleugh:
I wish that Jason's fleece
With him may still appear,
And that his flock would change
Their coats twelve times a year.

Dedicated to that worthy and generous gentleman, John Scot. *appearand of* Headshaw.

I Thought four and twenty shepherds swain,
 In my dream I did see,
Whereof I have dedicated one of them to thee;
John Grieve of Garwald a right honest one,
Which relieves the poor, and proves a Christian man;

And with his small substance he is well content,
Though in late times he prov'd a puritant.
I wish his fleeces be no worse,
Than Jason's fleeces was in Greece.

Dedicated to the Right Reverend and truly pious, and vertuous generous gentleman, Mr Richard Scot, *Parson of* Askirk.

THESE lines, good Sir, I present to your hand,
Is a genealogy of the old family of Sinton,
Which your self doth represent I know,
Except your nephew the Laird of Bonraw:
It is four hundred winters past in order,
Since that Buckcleugh was warden in the border;
A son he had at that same tide,
Which was so lame could neither run nor ride,
The Laird wist not what to do with him,
For Border service he was fit for none;
At his place cal'd Scotstoun,
He did there remain,
Four ages, or he went to Mordistoun;
And since he went, I can make appear,
It is more nor three hundred year:
John his lam'd son,
If my author speak true,
He sent him to St. Mungo's in Glasgow,
Where he remain'd a scholar's time,
Then married a wife according to his mind,
And betwixt them two was procreat,
Both sons and daughters of the name of Scot;
What time his posterity did there remain,
My author says, to the third generation;
Yet from that stock there sprung a man,
That was the Archbishop's chamberlain.

A quick mettel'd little man,
For which they call'd him Wat the Ratten :
This worthy Ratten did begin,
When Robert call'd Fern-year was Scotland's king ;
The bishop lov'd Wat well enough,
And recommended him to Buckclengh,
His chamberlain he did continue still,
And at the Burn-foot in Aill,
He built both kill and mill,
Then down the water he sought with speed,
And married Head-shaw's daughter,
Her name was Short Reid ;
And betwixt them two was procreat,
Head-shaw, Askirk, Sinton, and Glack ;
George was the first did Sinton's sweet knows flock,
He married Turnbul's daughter,
The knight of Falshope ;
Walter his son was call'd a pretty man,
He married with Scot the Laird of Hassindean ;
John, Walter's son, I have heard relation,
Married the Laird of Riddel's daughter,
And died without succession ;
Walter succeeded his brother John,
And married a daughter of the Laird of Johnston ;
Then George he was Walter's son,
He married Scot daughter to the Laird of Roberton;
This George was the very man
That was father to Sinton, Whiteslade, and Hardin,
For Walter he was George's son,
The elder brother of William of Hardin ;
This Walter Scot ye's understand,
He married Cockburn daughter of Henderland,
And betwixt them they got one only son,
The lady died when she was young ;

Their son Walter did to Riddel ride,
And took the Laird's daughter to his bride;
His father Walter was not an old man,
He married another daughter of Riddel's then,
And left Sinton unto his son;
And then in Whiteslade he sat down,
Betwixt him and Margaret Riddel was procreat
Twelve bairns that was all married;
Robert of Whiteslade was their first son,
And William of Huntly was his brother-german,
James of Satchels he was niest,
And Thomas of Whithaugh-bray made up the messe.
The eight daughters I'le let you ken,
The eldest was the lady Black-Ormston,
So was the Lady Langlands, and the Lady Tostturnbul;
The lady Ailmour she was next,
And the good wife of the Fanash,
And the Lady Chapel Middelmiss;
The youngest I have almost forgot,
She was first married to Philip of Kirk-up,
He was a brother to Robert of Thirleston;
Then she was married to Walter Scot of the Wall,
But to neither of them she bore children;
Then Alexander Chisholm of Park-hill did her gain,
And to him she bore twelve or thirteen bairns.
  Now my wearied muse, thou hast been long astray,
These are the first Whiteslade's posterity;
Now to George Howcoat I must return,
He was young Walter of Sinton's son,
A brave house-keeper, a worthy man,
He married Adimston, daughter to the Laird of Ednem;
Then Walter Scot was George Howcoat's son,
He married Douglass a daughter of Whittinghame,
And George his son a hopeful lad,
He married Gladstains daughter to the Laird of Dode,

                                                         There

There was procreat betwixt these two,
Good Mr George Scot, the Laird of Bon-raw;
George of Bonraw married was
To Douglas a brother-daughter of Cavers,
And there is procreat betwixt them twa,
This present young Laird of Bon-raw:
Most Reverend Sir, I hope you'l pardon me,
For waiding so deep in your genealogie:
If any man think he can amend it,
Poor Wattie Scot shall never be offended.

MY noble friends, at you I aim,
And of myself I do complain,
To all bad vices I've been bent,
And yet there's small amendement;
The Devil, the Flesh, the World, doth me oppose,
And are my mighty and my mortal foes;
The devil and flesh doth draw me still,
The world on wheels run after with good will;
For that which I the world may justly call,
I mean the lower globe terrestrial,
Is as the devil, and an whore doth please,
Drawn here and there, and every where with ease;
These that their lives to vertue here do frame,
Are in the world, but yet not of the same;
Some such there are, who neither flesh nor devil,
Can willfully draw on to any evil;
But for the world, as it's the world you see,
It runs on wheels, and they the palfrey be;
Which emblem to the reader doth display,
The devil, the flesh, do run both swift away,
The shrewd insnared world do follow fast,
Till all into perdition's pit be cast:

Let no man be offended, or think I do him wrong,
In comparing of the gentry unto a shepherd swain;
Many ages past a shepherd was of such dignity,
That gentry he surpast and best nobility;
Cain and Abel brethren were in the first age of man,
The elder was a husbander, the younger a shepherd swain;
The younger offer'd sacrifice to please the High Majesty,
The elder was a murderer, given to all villany;
Some shepherds past were kings at last,
So were never husbandmen;
Generals, conquerors, and emperors,
They have been shepherds swains:
The renown of a shepherd swain
Doth reach unto the sky,
The Charles-Wain signifies the same
To the mariners on the sea;
When you have read and understood my mind,
I hope your wonted favours I shall find;
In spight of railing baseness whose lewd tongues
Are Satan's instruments for slandrous wrongs;
A thousand rim of paper it would not contain,
To justifie the worthy shepherd swain:
Much hath the Church our mother propagated,
By venerable fathers works translated:
St Jerom, Gregory, Ambrose, Augustine,
St Basil, Beries, Cyprian, Constantine,
Eusebius, Epiphanius, and Origen,
Ignatius, and Lactantius, (reverend men)
Good Luther, Calvin, learned Zwinglius,
Melancton, Beza, Orcalampadus;
These, and a world more that I can recite,
Their labours would have slept in endless night,
But that in paper they preserv'd have been,
And instruct us to shun death, hell, and sin.

Past'ral.

How should we know the change of monarchies,
The Assyrian and the Persian empires,
Great Alexander's long small lasting glory,
Or Rome's high Caesar often changing story;
How should chronologies of kings be known,
Of either others countries or our own:
Shepherds have been priests, and shepherds have been kings,
And shepherds have been emperors, as my muse sings,
Which makes me to compare
The worthy name of Scot
To shepherds and to shepherds swain,
For they flocks and lands have got.
I would have none think these I call shepherd swain,
Is all the name of Scot, and that there's none but them,
There's forty eight that I have set apart,
All landed gentlemen that live upon their rent;
And for the shepherds swains, I have dedicate them,
Each one to a gentleman of that same name,
All landed gentlemen, that are infeft and seiz'd,
In five month in the year they pay the king his fee;
All besides burgers in city and in town,
That number heretors of respect and renown:
And for the fourty eight that live upon their rent,
Unto the reader I'm minded to relate,
Because I have not nominate them in fore-time,
I hear rehearse them in my following rime.

   Sir Francis Scot of Mengertoun, he hath a good state,
Although he be but young in years, he is knight baronet;
And John Scot of Sinton he is a pretty man,
He outstrips in wisdom any man I ken;
Headshaw and Burnfoot into the water of Ale,
They are both gentlemen, they dwell in Tiviotdale;
Chappel's a gentleman, Lochthirlston's another,
And Gladswood he's the same old Gallowshiels's brother:

                                                   The

The Laird of Langshaw him I have no mind to flee,
He is a gentleman, and is of kin to me;
The laird of Lochquharret he lives in good report,
So likewise doth the laird of good Hundelshope;
The laird of Langhope is a very young man,
But the laird of Broad-meadows is both great and strong;
Into Annandale three lairds of Scots there be,
Heuk, Bagra, and the laird of Gillisbie;
In Esdail-muir there does two lairds remain,
The laird of Johnstoun and laird of Devingtoun:
I'm now for Tiviotdale, if the fates do please,
And not miss the laird of the Mirrinies;
And the Laird of Harwood is a pretty man,
As is any in the south of them that I do ken;
The laird of Glack he may not be omitted,
He sold the lands of Gaudilands long ere he got it;
The laird of Alton-crafts I know him well enough,
The last lineal male branch that's sprung of Buckcleugh;
The laird of Whitoch I do him well know,
He is representative of the old family of Headshaw;
The laird of Caudhouse he is but a brood,
He is represeutative to the old house of Howfoord;
Three lairds all Scots I must exprime,
Tandlaw, Gallalaw, and Clarilaw's their name;
The laird of Bonraw, a very young man,
The representative of the old family of Sinton;
The laird of Newton he is a gentleman of note,
So is the laird of Alton on Tiviot's burnfoot;
The laird of Brierie-yard I cannot him refer,
Nor yet the Laird of Winns, nor laird of Boonchaster;
Scots-Tarbet and Ardross, they are lairds in the north,
But sprung from the loins of Haining in the south;
Bevely and Hallyards I had almost forgot,
They descended from Lawrence Scot Advocate;

The

The laird of Carnwath mill he is a gentleman,
And the representative of the old house of Bonnitoun;
There's another Bonnitoun into West-Lothian,
But I believe he be of Clarkinton's kind;
The laird of Deans-houses he is a gentleman,
Descended from the house of Gaudilands;
The laird of Chappel-know I need him not explain,
Through Tiviotdale he's known a gentleman;
The laird of Lies, if that ye wou'd him knaw;
He is brother to the laird of Clarilaw;
The laird of Clarklands is a gentleman indeed,
From his youth he has been a souldier bred;
John Scot a quarter master, sometime in command,
He married the heretrix of Clarklands;
Betwixt them two was procreat
That French Scots souldier, call'd William Scot:
The laird of Lethen, and the laird of Vogrie,
From the South they have their pedegree.
Here's an hundred and ten heretors of credit and renown,
All gentlemen, besides burgesses in towns,
And for every one of these five score,
Of the worthy name of Scot there's above a hundred more,
Which the number of ten thousand doth exceed,
In the forrest and Tiviotdale on the south side of Tweed,
All of one kindred into that country side;
I mean not the spacious nation long and wide,
But from one root these worthy branches sprang
Like Jacob's seed, when they to Egypt came:
I wish Apollo from great Etlas mountain
Assist them with his grace to fulfil their fountain;
That virtue, love, and grace, amongst them ever grow,
And that their fountain still may overflow.
Like trees in wood, some great, some small,
So is our heretors, yet gentlemen all;

There's many moe that to me is not known,
For never a man to me a single one has shown,
If I should pick from burgh or stot,
Landed gentlemen of the name of Scot,
Although it unto me would be a cumber,
Yet I could have added fourty to the number;
An hundred heritors of one name,
The like in Scotland I've not seen.
When Walter Earl of Buckcleugh he did to Holland wain,
There went with him a hundred gentlemen of that name,
For besides privat souldiers these did gang,
But friends and relations to attend his own person;
If he had been alive in the bygone toublesome time,
He might have raised a thousand, all of his own name;
And never a man been threatned by force,
But all voluntiers for foot and horse;
My verse is honest, true, seemly and mild,
My muse shall wade through dirt and not be fil'd;
The sun on loathsome dunghill shines as well,
As on fair flowers that have a fragrant smell;
The air, by which we live, doth every where
Breathe still alike, upon the rich and poor;
The sea bears many an old despised ship,
Yet on the sea the best ship doth but float;
And earth allows to call his scatter'd brood,
Food, cloathes, and lodging, either good or bad;
Yet sun, air, sea, and earth, thinks it disgrace,
For any bounty which they give the base;
Even so my muse free from all foul intents,
Doth take example from the elements;
Yet will I not my sense nor meaning mar,
With terms obscure, nor phrases fetcht from far,
Or will I any way equivocat,
With words sophistical or intricat;

Small eloquence men must expect from me,
My schollarship will name things as they be;
I may set out this little book indeed,
Yet cannot write, and little thing can read:
And now I fear I have done wrong,
In calling my friends shepherds swain,
So many sorts of shepherds constantly do grow,
That where there is no shepherds it is hard to know;
Cast but your eyes upon the man of Rome,
That stiles himself the head of Christendom.
Christ's universal vicar and vicegerent,
In whom fools think the truth is inherent,
That he can souls to heaven or hell prefer,
And being full of errors, cannot err;
Although his witchcraft a thousand have imbrac'd,
Yet he'll be call'd the Lieutenant to Christ,
Who by that false Conventicle of Trent,
Made laws that neither God nor good men meant,
Commanding worshipping of stone and stocks,
Of reliques, dead mens bones, and senseless blocks;
From which adultery, painted adulation,
Men worse than stock or block must seek salvation.
Great Julius Cesar was so free and common,
And call'd a husband unto every woman;
Proculus Emperor (the story says)
Deflowr'd an hundred maids in fifteen days:
If all be true that poets use to write,
Hercules lay with fifty in one night;
When Heliogabulus Rome's scepter sway'd,
And all the world his lawless laws obey'd,
He in his court caus'd stews be made,
Whereas (*cum privilegio*) whores did trade,
He invited two and twenty of his friends,
And kindly to each one a whore he lends;

To

To set whores free that then in bondage lay,
A mighty mass of money he did pay;
He in one day gave to each whore in Rome
A ducat, a large and ill bestowed sum;
He made orations unto whores, and said,
They were his souldiers, his defence and aid;
And in his speech he shew'd his wits acute,
Of sundry forms of bawdry to dispute;
And after giving unto every whore,
For listening to his tale three ducats more;
With pardon unto all and liberty,
That would be whores within his monarchy,
And yearly pensions he freely gave,
To keep a regiment of whores most brave;
And oft he had, when he in progress went,
Of whores, bawds, pandresses, such a rabblement,
Six hundred waggons, as histories reports,
Attended only by those brave consorts:
This was a royal whore-master indeed,
A special benefactor in their need;
But none since Heliogabulus deceast,
I think the world with whores is so increast;
That if it had an Emperor as mad,
He might have twice so many as he had.
Here I leave whores and whore-masters,
Unto the man of Rome;
And to the worthy shepherd swain,
I presently return.

 Because I know, and presently maintain,
That he that laboureth to be a worthy man,
May with a better conscience sleep in bed,
Than with the gout and gravel as I'm speed,
Yet to keep my health from falling to decay,
When I am most tormented, I terrifie,

A thousand times it is more pains then dead,
I'm sure it by antiquity hath stood,
Since the world's drowning universal flood;
Though my wits be like my purse, but bare,
With poets I dare not compare,
Yet to dite verse, provided that they be,
No better skill'd in scholarship than I,
' And then come on as many as you will,
' And for a wager, I'l verse with them still;
Myself I liken to an untun'd vial,
For like a vial I'm in a case,
And whoso of my fortune makes a trial,
Shall like to me be strung and tuned base;
And treble troubles he shall never want:
But here's the period of my mischiefs all,
Though base and treble fortune did me grant,
And means, but yet alas it is too scant;
Yet to make up the musick, I'le venture a fall,
To the tenor in the Carset town-hall:
A poet rightly may be termed fit
An abstract or epitome of wit,
Or like a lute, that other pleasures breed,
Are sweet and strong their curious eyes to feed,
That scornfully distaste it, yet it's known,
It makes the hearers sport, but it self none:
A poet's like a taper burnt by night,
That wastes itself in giving others light;
A poet's the most fool beneath the skyes,
He spends his wit in making others wise;
Who, when they should their thankfulness return,
They pay him with disdain, contempt and scorn,
An independant is like a poet's purse;
For both do hate the cross, what cross is worse?

His holy hymns, and psalms for consolation,
For reprehension, and for contemplation;
And finally to show us our salvation,
The prophet Amos, unto whom the Lord
Reveal'd the sacred secrets of his word,
God rais'd him from the sheep-folds to foretell,
What plagues shall fall in sinful Israel;
True patience, pattern prince of his afflictions,
Most mighty tamer of his imperfections,
Whose guard was God, whose guide's the Holy Ghost,
Blest in his wealth, of whom sheep was the most;
Just Job's last riches doubled was again,
Who liv'd belov'd of God, admir'd of men:
The first of happy tidings on the earth,
Of our all only blessed Saviour's birth;
The glorious angels to the shepherds told,
As Luke the Evangelist doth unfold.
And, should my verse a little but decline,
To human stories, and leave divine;
There are some mighty princes I can name,
Whose breeding at the first from shepherds came;
Rome's founder Romulus was bred and fed
'Mongst shepherds, where his youthful days he led;
The Persian monarch Cyrus he did pass
His youth with shepherds, and a shepherd was;
The terror of the world, that famous man,
Who conquer'd kings, and over kingdoms ran,
His stile was, as some histories do repeat,
The Scythian shepherd, Tamerlane the Great;
'Tis such a title of preheminence,
Of reverence, and such high magnificence;
That David who so well his words did frame,
Did call our great Creator by that name;

Our

Our blest Redeemer, God's eternal son,
Whose only merits our salvation won,
He did the harmless name of shepherd take.
Apollo father of the sisters nine,
I crave thee, and inspire this muse of mine;
Thou that thy golden glory didst lay by,
As Ovid doth relate most wittily,
And in a shepherd's shape didst design to keep,
Thy love's beloved Adamus sheep;
And rural Pan thy help I do intreat,
That to the life thy praise I may repeat;
Of the contented life, and mighty stocks,
Are happy shepherds, and there harmless flocks;
But better thoughts my errours do controul,
For an offence most negligent and foul,
In this involving like an heathen man;
Help helpless from Apollo, or from Pan;
When as the subject which I have in hand,
Is almost infinit, as stars, or sand;
Grac'd with antiquity upon record,
In the eternal never-failing word;
There 'tis ingraven, true and manifest,
That sheep and shepherds were both best and blest;
I therefore invocat his gracious aid,
Of him whose mighty hand hath all things made;
I Israel's Great shepherd humbly crave,
That his assur'd assistance I may have;
That my unlearned muse no verse compile,
Which may be impious, prophane, or vile;
And though, through ignorance or negligence,
My poor intention fall into offence,
I do implore that boundless grace of his,
Not strictly to regard what is amiss;

But

But unto me belongeth all the blame,
And all the glory be unto his name;
Yet as my book is verse, so men may know,
I might some fictions and allusions show:
Some shreds or remnants, reliques, or some scrapes,
The muses may inspire me with perhaps,
Which taken literally, as't lyes may seem,
And so mis-understanding may misdeem.
Of sheep therefore before to work I fall,
To show the shepherds first original;
These that the best records will read and mark,
Shall find just Able was a patriarch,
Our father Adam's second son a prince,
As great as any man begotten since;
And in his function he a shepherd was,
And so his mortal pilgrimage did pass;
And in the sacred text it is compil'd,
That he that's Father of the Faithful stil'd,
Did as a shepherd live upon th' increase
Of sheep, until his days on earth did cease;
And in these times it was apparent then,
Abram and Abel both were noble-men;
The one obtain'd the title righteously,
For his unfeigned serving the most high;
He first did offer sheep, which on record,
Was sacrifice accepted of the Lord;
He was, before the infant world was rype,
The church's figure, and our Saviour's type;
A murdered martyr, who, for serving God,
Did first of all feel persecution's rod;
And Abram was in account so great,
Abimelech his friendship did intreat,
Faith's patern, and obedience sample he,
Like stars, or sand, was in prosperity.

In him the nations of the earth were blest,
And now his bosom figures heavenly rest;
His sheep almost past numbering multiplied,
And when as he thought Isaac should have died,
Then by the Almightie's mercies, love, and grace,
A sheep from out the bush supplied the place;
Lot was a shepherd, Abram's brother son,
And such great favour from his God he won,
That Sodom could not be consum'd with fire,
Till he and his did out of it retire;
They felt no vengence for their foul offence,
Till righteous Lot was quite departed hence;
And Jacob, as the Holy Ghost doth tell,
Who afterward was called Israel,
Who wrestled with his God, and to his fame
Obtain'd a name, and blessing for the same;
He under Laban was a shepherd long,
And suffer'd from him much ungrateful wrong;
For Rachel and Leah he did bear,
The yoke of servitude full twenty year:
He was a patriarch, a prince of might,
Whose wealth in sheep was almost infinite;
His twice six sons, as holy writ describes,
Who were the famous fathers of twelve tribes,
Were for the most part shepherds, and such men,
Whose like the world shall ne're contain again;
Young Joseph 'mongst the rest especially,
A constant mirror of true chastity,
Who was in his afflictions of behaviour
A mortal type of his immortal Saviour,
And truth his Mother Rachel doth express,
To be her Father Laban's Shepherdess.
Meek Moses whom the Lord of Hosts did call,
To lead his people out of Ægypt's thrall,

Whose power was so much as none before,
Or since his time hath any man's been more,
Within the sacred text it plainly appears,
That he was Jethro's shepherd twenty years;
Heroick David, Jesse's youngest son,
Whose acts immortal memory hath won,
Whose valiant vigour did in pieces tear
A furious lyon, and a ravenous bear,
Who arm'd with faith, and fortitude alone,
Slew great Goliah with a slinging stone;
Whose victories the people sang most plain,
Saul hath a thousand, he ten thousand slain,
He from the sheep-fold came to be a King,
Whose fame for ever through the world shall ring;
He was another type of that Most High,
That was, and is, and evermore shall be,
For our protection and his mercies sake.
Those that will read the sacred text, and look
With diligence throughout that heavenly book,
Shall find the Ministers have epithets,
And named angels, stewards, watch-men, lights,
All builders, husbandmen, and stars that shine,
Inflamed with the light that is divine;
And with these names, within that book compil'd
They with the stile of shepherds are instil'd;
Thus God the seer and son the scriptures call,
Both sheperds mystical and literal;
And by similitudes comparing, do
All kings and church-men bear that title too.
Wise and unscruteable, omniscient,
Eternal, gracious, and omnipotent,
In love, in justice, mercy, and in might,
In honour, power, and glory infinite,
In works, in words, in every attribute;
Almighty, all commanding, absolute,

For whoso notes the letters of the name,
Jehovah, shall perceive within the same,
The vowels of all tongues included be,
So hath no name, that e'er was named but He.
And I have heard some scholars make relation,
That H is but a breathing aspiration,
A letter that may be left out and spared,
Whereby is clearly to our sight declared,
That great Jehovah may be written true,
With only vowels, a, e, i, o, u.
And that there is no word but this,
That hath them alone, but only this,
So that the heaven, with all the mighty host
Of creatures there, earth, sea, or any coast,
Or climat, any fish, or fowl, or beast,
Or any of his works, the most and least,
Or thoughts, or words, or writing with the pen,
Or deeds that are accomplished by men,
But have some of these letters in them all,
And God alone hath all in general:
By which we see according to his will,
He is in all things, and does all things fill;
And all things said or done he hath ordain'd,
Some part of his great name's therein contain'd;
All future, present, and all past things, seeing;
In him we live, and move, and have our being;
Almighty, all, and all in every where,
Eternal, in whom change cannot appear;
Immortal, who made all things mortal else,
Omnipotent, whose power all power excels;
United three in one, and one in three,
Jehovah, unto whom all glory be.
  Besides the learned poets of all times,
Have chanted out their praises in pleasant rhimes,

The harmless lives of rural shepherd swains,
And beauteous shepherdesses on the plains,
In odes, in roundelays, and madrigals,
In sonnets, and in well penn'd post'rals,
They have recorded most delightfully
Their loves, their fortunes, and felicity;
And sure if in this low terrestrial round,
Plain honest happiness is to be found,
It with the shepherds is remaining still.
Because they have least power to do ill:
And whilst they on their feeding flocks attend,
They have the least occasions to offend;
Ambition, pomp, and hell-begotten pride,
And damned adulation they deride,
The complementel-flatt'ry of kings courts
Is never intermix'd amids their sports;
They seldom envy at each others state,
Their love and fear is God's, the Devil's their hate;
In weighty business they not mar, or make,
And cursed bribes they neither give nor take;
They are not guilty as some great men are,
To undo their merchant and embroiderer;
Nor is't a shepherd's trade by night or day,
To swear themselves, and never pay;
He's no state-plotting Matchivilian,
Or project-monger Monopolitan;
He hath no tricks or wiles to circumvent,
Nor fears he when there comes a parliament;
He never wears cap, nor bends his knee,
To feed contention with an advocate's fee;
He wants the art to cog, cheat, swear and ly,
Nor fears the gallows, nor the pillory,
Nor cares he if great men be fools or wise,
If honour fall, and base dishonour rise:

Let fortune's mounted minions sink or swim,
He never breaks his brains, all's one to him:
He's free from fearful curses of the poor,
And lives and dies content with less or more.
He doth not waste the time as many use,
His good Creator's creatures to abuse,
In drinking such ungodly healths to some,
The veriest canker-worms in Christendom;
My Lord Ambition, and my Lady Pride,
Shall with this quaffing not be magnified,
Nor for their sakes shall he carouse and feast,
Until from man he turn worse than a beast;
Whereby he 'scapes vain oaths and blasphemy,
And surfeits fruits of drunken gluttony;
He 'scapes occasion unto lust's pretence,
And so escapes the pox by consequence;
Thus doth he hate the parator and proctor,
The apothecary, chirurgeon and doctor,
Whereby he this perogative may have,
To hold while he be laid into his grave;
Whilst many that his betters far have been,
Will very hardly hold the lying in:
Crook, blanket, terkit, tarrier-like, call'd Crouse,
Shall breed no jars into the Parliament-house.
Thus shepherds live, and thus they end their lives,
Adorn'd and grac'd with these perogatives,
And when he dies, he leaves no wrangling heirs,
To law, till all be spent, and nothing theirs,
Peace and tranquitity was all his life,
And dead, his goods shall breed no cause of strife.
Thus shepherds have no places, means or times,
To fall into these hell-deserving crimes,
Which courtiers, lawyers, tradesmen, men of arms,
Commit unto their souls and bodies harms.

And from the shepherds now I turn my stile,
To sundry sort of sheep another while;
The lambs that in the Jew's passover died,
Were figures of the Lamb that's crucified;
And Esay doth compare our heavenly food
To a sheep, which dumb before the shearer stood,
Whose death and merits did this title win,
The Lamb of God, which freed the world from sin;
The anagram of Lamb is blame and blame,
And Christ the Lamb upon him took our blame;
His precious blood God's heavy wrath did calm,
'Twas the only balme for sin to cure the same;
All power and praise and glory be therefore
Ascribed to the Lamb for evermore:
And in the fourscore psalm we read,
That like a sheep our God doth Joseph lead;
Again of us he such account doth keep,
That of his pasture we are called sheep;
And every day we do confess almost,
That we have err'd and stray'd like sheep that's lost
Our Saviour that hath bought our souls so dear,
Hath said, his sheep his voice will only hear;
And thrice did Christ unto St Peter call,
In which he spake to his disciples all,
If ye do love me, feed my sheep, (quoth he)
And feed my lambs, if ye love me;
Moreover, in the final judgement day,
There is the right hand, and the left hand way,
Whereas the sheep he to himself doth gather,
With saying, Come, ye blessed of my father, &c.
And to the goats in his consuming ire,
He bids depart to everlasting fire.
Thus our Redeemer and his whole elect,
The name of sheep had ever in respect,

And the comparison holds reference,
To profit, and to harmless innocence;
For of all beasts that ever were or are,
None can for goodness with a sheep compare;
Indeed for bone and burden I must grant,
He's much inferiour to the elephant;
The dromedary, camel, horse, and ass,
For load and carriage doth the sheep surpass;
Strong Taurus, Eunuch's son, the labouring ox,
The stately staig, the bobtail'd crafty fox;
These, and all rav'nous beasts of prey must yield,
Unto the sheep the honour of the field;
I could recount the names of many more,
The lyon, unicorn, the bear, and boar,
The wolf, the tyger, the renoscerat,
The leopard, and a number more I wot;
But all these greedy beasts great Ovid's pen,
Calls metamorphos'd into men:
For beast to beast afford more conscience can,
And much less cruelty than man to man;
I'le therefore let such beasts be as they be,
For fear they kick and snarl at me.
Unto the sheep again my muse doth flee,
For honest safety and commoditie,
He with his flesh and fleece doth cleed and feed,
All languages and nations, good and bad.
What can it more than die, that we may live,
And ev'ry year to us a liv'ry give?
'Tis such a bounty, and the charge so deep,
That nothing can defray the charge but sheep;
For, should the world want sheep but five whole year,
Ten thousand millions would want cloaths to wear:
And wer't not for the flesh of this kind beast,
The world might fast when it doth ofted feast;

There's nothing doth unto a sheep pertain,
But 'tis for man's commodity and gain;
For men to men so much untrusty are,
To lie, to couzin, to forswear and swear,
That oaths, and passing words, and joining hands,
Is like assurance written in the sands;
To make men keep their words, and in end this
The silly sheep-skin turn'd to parchment is;
There's many a wealthy man whose whole estate
Lyes more in parchment than in coin or plate,
Indentures, leases, evidences, wills,
Bonds, contracts, records, obligations, bills,
With these, although the sheep-skin be but weak,
It binds men strongly that they dare not break:
But if a man eats spiders now and then,
The oil of parchment cures him oft again,
And what rare stuffs which in the world are fram'd
Can be in value like to parchment nam'd?
The richest cloath of gold that can be found,
A yard of it was ne're worth five hundred pound;
And I have seen two foot of sheep-skin drest,
Which have been worth ten thousand pound at least;
A piece of parchment well with ink laid over,
Helps many gallant to a starving power;
Into the merchant it some faith doth strick,
It gives the silkman hope of no dislike;
The taylor it with charity assails,
It thrusts him last betwixt his bill and vails;
And by these means a piece of parchment can
Patch up and make a gull a gentleman:
The nature of it very strange I find,
It's much like physick it can loose and bind;
It's one man's freedom and another's loss,
And like the Pope it doth both bind and loose;

And

And as the ram and ewe doth fructifie,
And ev'ry year a lamb doth multiply,
So doth a sheep-skin bound make money breed,
And procreat, as seed doth spring from seed.
   Thus is a sheep-skin prov'd the only ty,
And stay whereon a world of men rely,
' Which holds a crew of earth-worms in more aw,
' Than both the tables of the sacred law :
Past number I could functions name,
Who as it's parchment live upon the same ;
But it's sufficient this small homely touch ;
Should more be writ, my book would swell too much.
Now for the ram, the ewe, the lamb and weather,
I'le touch their skins as they are touch'd to leather ;
And made in purses, pouches, laces, strings,
Gloves, points, books, covers, and ten thousand things ;
And many tradesmen live and thrive thereby,
Which if I would I more could amplify ;
Their guts serve instruments, which sweetly sound,
Their dung is best to make most fruitful ground,
Their hoofs burnt will most venomous serpents kill,
Their grated horns are good for poison still,
Their milk makes cheese that has no fellow,
The best that's made in Etrick or in Yarrow ;
Their feet for the healthy or the sick,
Drest as they should be, are good meat to pick ;
The cook and butcher with the joints do gain,
And poor folks eat the gedder, head, and brain ;
And though all wise mens judgements will allow,
A sheep to be much lesser than a cow.
Now for the honour of the valiant ram,
If I were learn'd more treble than I am,
Yet could I not sufficiently express,
His wondrous worth and excellent worthiness :

For by Astronomers it is verified,
How that the Ram in heav'n is styllified,
And of the twelve is plac'd head sign of all,
Where Sols keep first his equinoctial;
For having with the Bull drunk April showers,
And with the Twins doth deck the earth with flowers,
And scorch't the Crab in June with burning beams,
Made July's Lyon chaff with fiery gleams,
In August solace to the Virgin given,
With Balance in September made time even,
October Scorpion with decling course,
And passing by December's Archers force;
Then having past November's frozen gate,
He next to Janus wat'ry sign doth float,
He to the Lentil sign in February,
And so bright Phoebus ends his year's figarie;
Then to the Ram in March in his carrier,
He mounts, on which this sonnet's written here.
Now chearful Sol in his illustrious car,
To glade the earth his journey 'gins to take,
And now his glorious beams he doth unbar,
While's absence marr'd, his presence now doth make;
Now he earths weeping 'gins to dry,
With Eolus breath and his bright heavenly heat,
March-dust like clouds through air doth march and fly,
And seeming trees, and plants now life doth get;
Thus when the world's eye-dazler takes his time,
At the celestial Ram then winter's done,
And then dame nature doth her livery spin,
Of flowers and fruits, which all the earth puts on;
Thus when Apollo doth to Aries come,
The earth is freed from winter's martyrdom.
Thus have I prov'd the Ram a lucky sign,
Wherein sun, earth, and heaven, and air combine,

To have their universal comfort harl'd,
Upon the time of our decaying world;
With twelve signs each man's body is govern'd,
And Aries of the Ram doth rule the head;
Then are the judgements foolish, fond and base,
That take the name of ram-head in disgrace;
'Tis honour for the head to have the name,
Derived from the ram that rules the same;
' And that the ram doth rule the head I know,
' For ev'ry almanack the same doth show.
    From whence such men may gather this relief,
That though a ram-head may be cause of grief;
Yet nature hath this remedy found out,
They should have lyons hearts to bear it out;
And to defend and keep the head from harm,
The anagram of ram I find is arm;
Thus is a ram-head arm'd against all fear;
He needs no helmet, nor no head-piece wear;
To speak more in the plural number rams,
It yields significk war-like anagrams;
The ram is Mars, Mars is the god of war;
And ram is arms, arms war's munitions are;
And from the fierce encounters which they make,
Our tilts and turneys did beginning take;
For as the rams retire, and meet with rage,
So men do in their warlike equipage;
And long ere pouder from hell's damn'd den,
Was monstrously produced to murder men,
The ram, an engine call'd a ram did teach,
To batter down a wall, or make a breach;
And now some places of defence 'gainst shot,
Have from the ram the name of rampiers got;
First warlike trumpets that I e're heard nam'd,
At Jericho were all of ram-horns fram'd,

                                                            For

For at the ram-horns trumpets fearful blast,
Their curled walls were suddenly down cast:
Thus is the ram with many vertues stor'd,
And was in Ægypt for a god ador'd;
And like a captain he the flock doth lead,
As fits their general, their prince, and head.
Thus have I prov'd a sheep a beast of price,
Clean and reputed, fit for sacrifice;
And sleeping, waking, early, or else late,
It still doth chew the cud and ruminat:
Of all beasts in the world's circumference,
For meekness, profit, and for innocence,
I have approv'd a sheep most excellent,
That with least cost doth give most content;
There's such instinct of nature in the lamb,
By bleating it 'mongst thousands knows the dame,
For which the name of agnoscendo knowing,
Is given to a lamb it's knowledge showing.
And now from solid prose I will abstain,
To pleasant poetry, and mirth again;
The fables of the golden fleece began,
Because sheep wool yields store of gold to men;
For he that hath great store of wooly fleeces,
May when he please have store of golden pieces:
Thus many a poor man dying hath left a son,
That hath transform'd the fleece to gold like Jason.
And here's a mystery profound and deep,
There's sundry sorts of mutton are no sheep;
Lac'd mutton, which let out themselves to hyre
Like hakneys, will be fir'd before they tyre;
The man or men which for such mutton hunger
Are by their corporations mutton-mongers,
Which is a brother-hood too large and great,
That if they had a hall, I would intreat

To be their clerk, or keeper of accounts,
To shew them unto what their charge amounts.
My brain in numbring then would grow so quick,
I should be master of arithmetic;
All states, degrees, and trades, both bad and good,
Afford some members of this brother-hood;
Great therefore, then, must be their multitude,
When every man may to the trade intrude.
It is no freedom, yet these men are free;
No savers, but most liberal spenders be;
For this is one thing that doth them bewitch,
That by their trading they wax seldom rich;
The value of this mutton so set forth,
The flesh doth cost more than the broth is worth;
They all are ews, yet are exceeding ramish,
And will be dainty fed, who ever famish;
Nor are they marked for any man, or no man,
As mine, or thine, but every man is common;
Fine heads, and necks, and breasts they yield some store,
But scarcely one good liver in ninescore;
The liver being bad, it's understood,
The veins are fill'd with putrified blood,
Which makes them subject to the scab, and then
They prove most dangerous diets unto men;
And then the proverb proves no ly or mock,
One scabbed sheep's enough to spoil a flock.
But yet, for all this, there's many a gull,
Loves mutton well, dips not his bread i'th' wool;
And were a man put to his choice to keep,
'Tis said a shrew is better than a sheep;
But if a man be yoked with such an ewe,
She may be both a scabbed sheep and shrew;
And he that is so mach't, his life may well
Be compared unto an earthly hell.

But of my theam which I wrote of before,
I at this mutton must have one cut more;
These kind of sheep have all the world o'ergrown,
And seldom do wear fleeces of their own;
For they from sundry men their pellets can pull,
Whereby they keep themselves as warm as wool;
Besides in colours, and in shapes they wear,
Quite from all profitable sheep contrair;
White, black, green, tawny, purple, red, and blue,
Beyond the rain-bow, for the change of hew;
Came soon like an alteration,
But that bare air they cannot live upon;
The moon's mutation not more manifold,
Silk, velvet, tissue, cloath, and cloath of gold.
These are the sheep that golden fleeces wear,
Who rob themselves with others wool or hair;
And it may be 'twas such a beast and fleece,
Which Jason brought from Colchos into Greece;
Were it no more but so I dare be bold
To think the land doth many Jason's hold,
Who never durst to pass a dangerous wave,
Yet may with ease such golden fleeces have.
Too much of one thing is good for nothing, they say,
I'le therefore take this needless dish away;
For should I too much of lac'd mutton write,
I may overcome my reader's stomach quite;
Once more unto the good sheep I'le retire,
And so my book shall to it's end expire;
Although it be not found in antient writers,
I find all mutton-eaters are sheep-biters;
And in some places, I have heard and seen,
That currish sheep-biters they have hanged been;
' If any kind of tyke should snarle or whinnie,
' Or bite or worry this poor sheep of mine,

' Why?

' Why ? Let them bark, or bite, and spend their breath,
' I'le never wish them a sheep-biter's death;
My sheep should have them know their innocence,
Shall live in spight of their malevolence;
I wish they keep themselves and me from pain,
And bite such sheep, as cannot bite again;
For if they snap at mine, I have a tongue,
That like a trusty dog shall bite again:
And in conclusion, this I humbly crave,
That every one the honesty may have,
That when our frail mortality is past,
We may be the good shepherd's sheep at last.
When all things were as wrapt in sable night,
And ebeon'd darkness muffled up the night,
When neither sun, nor moon, nor stars had shin'd,
And when no fire, no water, earth nor wind,
No harvest, autumn, winter, nor no spring,
No bird, beast, fish, nor any creeping thing,
When there was neither time, nor place, nor space,
And silence did the Chaos round embrace;
Then did the Arch-work-master of us all,
Creat this massie universal ball,
And with his mighty word brought all to pass,
Saying, but Let there be, and done it was;
Let there be day, night, water, earth, herbs, trees,
Let there be sun, moon, stars, fish, fowl that flies,
Beast of the field; he said, let there be;
All things were created, as we may see.
Thus every sensible and sensless thing,
The high Creator's word to pass did bring;
And as in viewing of his works he stood,
He said, that all things were exceeding good:
Thus having finish'd seas, and earth, and skyes,
Abundantly with all varieties,

Like a magnificent and sumptuous feast,
To th' intertainment of some welcome guest,
When beasts, and birds, and every living creature,
And the earth's fruits did multiply by nature;
Then did the Eternal Trinity betake
Itself to council, and said, Let us make,
Not let there be, as unto all things else;
But let us make man that the rest excells;
According to our image, let us make
Man; and then the Almighty red earth did take,
With which he formed Adam every limb,
And having made him, breathed life in him.
Lo thus the first man never was a child,
No way with sin original defil'd;
But with high super-natural understanding,
He over all the world had sole commanding;
Yet though to him the regency was given
As earth's leivetennant to the God of heaven,
Though he commanded all created things,
As deputy under the King of kings,
Though he so highly here was dignified,
To humble him, not to be puft with pride;
He could not brag nor boast of high-born birth,
For he was formed out of slime and earth;
No beast, fish, worm, fowl, herb, wood, stone, tree,
But are of a more antient house than he;
For they were made before him, which prove this,
That their antiquity is more than his.
Thus both himself, and his beloved spouse,
Are by creation of the younger house;
And whilst they liv'd in perfect holiness,
Their richest garments were bare nakedness,
True innocence were their chiefest weeds;
For righteousness no mask or vizard needs;

The royalist robes that our first parents had,
Was a free conscience with uprightness clad;
They needed not to shift, the cloaths they wore
Was nakedness, and they desir'd no more;
Until at last, that hell-polluting sin,
With disobedience sold their soul within;
And having lost their holiest perfection
They held their nakedness in imperfection;
Then being both asham'd, they both did frame,
Garments as weeds of their deserved shame:
Thus when as sin had brought God's curse on man,
Then shame to make apparel first began;
E're men had said most plain it does appear,
He neither did, nor needed cause menswear;
For his apparel did at first begin,
To be the robes of pennance for his sin;
Thus all the brood of Adam, and of Eve,
The true use of apparel may perceive;
That they are liveries, badges unto all,
Of our sins, and our Parents woeful fall;
Then more than mad the mad-brain'd people be,
Or else they see, and will not seem to see,
The same robes of pride that makes them swell,
Are tokens that our best deserts are Hell,
Much like unto a traitor to his king,
Which would his countrey into destruction bring,
Whose treacheries being prov'd apparently,
He by the law is justly judg'd to die;
And when the books for his deserved death,
A pardon comes, and gives him longer breath,
I think this man most madly would appear,
That would a halter in a glory wear,

Of life to be quite dis-inherited;
But if he should vain gloriously persist,
To make a rope of silk, or golden twist,
And wear, it's a more honourable show
Of his rebellion than course hemp or tow;
Might not men justly say he were an ass,
Triumphing that he once a villain was,
And that wears an halter for the nonce,
In pride that he deserv'd a hanging once.
Such with our Heavenly Father is the case,
Of our first parents, and their fruitful race;
Apparel is the miserable sign,
That we are traitors to our Lord divine,
And we like rebels still most pride do take,
In that which still most humble should us make;
Apparel is the prison for our sin,
Which most should shame, yet most we glory in;
Apparel is the sheet of shame, as it were;
For man apparel never did receive,
Till he eternal death deserv'd to have:
How vain it is for man, a clod of earth,
To boast of his progeny or birth,
Because perhaps his ancestors were good,
And sprung from royal or from noble blood;
Where vertues worth did in their minds inherit,
They enjoy'd their honour by desert and merit.
Great Alexander, king of Macedon,
Disdain'd to be his father Philip's son,
But he from Jupiter would be descended,
And as a god be honour'd and attended;
Yet when at Babylon he prov'd but a man,
His god-head ended foolish as't began;
There was in Cicily a proud physician,
Menecrates, and he through high ambition,

To be a god himself would needs prefer,
And would forsooth be deemed Jupiter;
King Dionysius making a great feast,
The fool god disguis'd to be a great beast;
Who by himself was at a table plac'd,
Because as god he should the more be grac'd;
The other guests themselves did feed and fill,
He at an empty table still sat still;
At last with humble low Sir Reverence,
A fellow came with fire and frankincense,
And offered to his god-ship, saying then,
Perfumes were fit for gods, and meat for men;
The god in anger raise incontinent,
Who laughed, and in hunger homeward went.
The Roman Emperor Domitian
Would be a god, was murdered by a man.
Caligola would be a god of wonders,
And counterfeit the lightening and the thunders,
Yet every real heavenly thunder crack,
This cateif in such fear and terror strake,
That he would quake, and shake, and hide his head
In any hole, or underneath his bed;
And when this godless god had many slain,
A Preband dasht out his ungodly brain:
And thus the Almighty still against pride doth frown,
And casts ambition headlong tumbling down.
Great Pompey would be all the world's superior,
And Caesar unto none would be inferior;
But as they both did live ambitiously,
So both of them untimeous deaths did die:
The one in Ægypt had his final fall,
The other murdered in the capital.
A number more examples are beside,
Which shows the miserable fall of pride:

For pride of state, birth, wisdom, beauty, strength,
And pride in any thing will fall at length :
But to be proud of garments that we wear,
Is the most foolish pride a heart can bear :
Know that of thine own thou doth possess,
Nothing but sin and woeful wretchedness :
A Christian's pride should only be in this,
When he can say, that God his father is ;
When grace and mercy well applied, afford
To make him brother unto Christ his Lord :
When he unto the Holy Ghost can say,
Thou art my schoolmaster whom I will obey.
When he can call the saints his fellows, and
Say to the angels for my guard you stand ;
This is a laudable and Christian pride,
To know Christ and to know him crucified ;
This is that meek ambition low aspiring,
Which all men should be earnest in desiring :
Thus to be proudly humble is the thing,
Which will us to the state of glory bring ;
But yet beware of pride hypocritical,
For pride in every thing will have a fall :
A lofty mind with lowly cap on knee,
Is humble pride and meek hypocrisie ;
As a great ship ill suited with small sail,
A Judas mean'd all mischief, cry'd all hail :
Like the humility of Absalom,
That sort of pride much dangers waits upon :
They are the couterfeit, God save you, Sirs,
That have their flatteries in particulars,
That courteously can hide their own intents.
Under varieties of complements ;
These vipers bend the knee, and kiss the hand,
And swear, sweet Sir, I am at your command :

And

And proudly make humility a screw,
To wring themselves into opinion's view:
Thus pride is hateful, dangerous and vile,
And shall itself at last itself beguile:
Thus pride is deadly sin, and sin brings shame,
Which here I leave to hell from whence it came.

SINCE the water of Ail Scots they are all chang'd and gone,
   Except brave Whitslade and Hardin,
And Satchels his estate is gone,
Except his poor designation,
Which never no man shall possess,
Except a Scot designed Satchels.
   Therefore begone my book, stretch forth thy wings and fly,
Amongst the nobles and gentility:
Thour't not to sell to scavingers and clowns,
But given to worthy persons of renown.
The number's few I've printed in regard
My charges have been great, and I hope reward;
I caus'd not print many above twelve score,
And the printers are engag'd that they shall print no more.

FINIS.

PUBLICATIONS OF THE

Scotish Literary Club,

INSTITUTED: M.DCCC.LXXVII.

SUBSCRIPTION FEE TWO GUINEAS.

No. I.

IN SMALL QUARTO, EMBELLISHED WITH A FINE FRONTISPIECE FROM A DRAWING BY CHARLES KIRKPATRICK SHARPE, HALF-BOUND MOROCCO WITH GILT TOP,

IMPRESSION LIMITED TO SIXTY COPIES,

THE WORKS OF ADAM PETRIE

(" The Scottish Chesterfield"),

Now first Collected, viz.— I. Rules of Good Deportment, or of Good Breeding. For the Use of Youth, 1720. II. Rules of Good Deportment for Church Officers; or, Friendly Advices to them, 1730. III. A Poem upon the Metaphor of Ministers being compared to Shepherds. Edited, with interesting Prefatory Remarks and Notices of ADAM PETRIE and THOMAS MAITLAND *(Lord Dundrennan)*, with a List of his Publications.

☞ THE RARITY OF THE WORKS OF ADAM PETRIE is well known to all Bibliomaniacs. He for some time acted as domestic Tutor in the family of SIR ROBERT SINCLAIR *of Stevenston, near Haddington.* It is known to have been the intention of SIR WALTER SCOTT to reprint PETRIE'S WORKS for the BANNATYNE CLUB.

No. II.

IN SMALL QUARTO, HALF-BOUND MOROCCO WITH GILT TOP,

IMPRESSION LIMITED TO FIFTY COPIES,

SCOT'S (CAPTAIN WALTER,

of Satchells, Roxburgh-Shire,)

METRICAL HISTORY of the FAMILIES of the NAME of SCOT and ELLIOT in the SHIRES of ROXBURGH and SELKIRK (IN TWO PARTS), gathered out of Ancient Chronicles, Histories, and Traditions of our Fathers, 1688-1776. Edited, with Prefatory Notices.

☞ THIS METRICAL HISTORY of the FAMILIES of the SCOTS and ELLIOTS preserves many curious Traditions respecting the Origin of several Branches of the Families in Roxburgh and Selkirk Shires.

THOMAS GEORGE STEVENSON, *Secretary,* 22 FREDERICK STREET, EDINBURGH.

www.ingramcontent.com/pod-product-compliance
Lightning Source LLC
Chambersburg PA
CBHW020257170426
43202CB00008B/408